# Kids, Computers, and Learning

## An Activity Guide for Parents

*Holly Poteete*

HomePage
Books

HomePage Books is an imprint of the
International Society for Technology in Education
EUGENE, OREGON • WASHINGTON, DC

# Kids, Computers, and Learning

## An Activity Guide for Parents

*Holly Poteete*

© 2010 International Society for Technology in Education

Director of Book Publishing: *Courtney Burkholder*
Acquisitions Editor: *Jeff V. Bolkan*
Production Editors: *Lynda Gansel, Tina Wells*
Production Coordinator: *Rachel Williams*

Graphic Designer: *Signe Landin*
Copy Editor: *Kristin Landon*
Proofreader: *Anna Drexler*
Cover & Book Design: *Kathy Sturtevant*

Library of Congress Cataloging-in-Publication Data

Poteete, Holly.
  Kids, computers, and learning : an activity guide for parents /
  Holly Poteete. — 1st ed.
     p. cm.
  ISBN 978-1-56484-265-7 (pbk.)
  1. Computer-assisted instruction.  2. Computers and children.
  3. Educational technology.  4. Cognitive styles in children.  I. Title.
  LB1028.5.P676 2010
  372.133'4—dc22

                                                                2010009195

First Edition
ISBN: 978-1-56484-265-7
Printed in the United States of America

**International Society for Technology in Education (ISTE)**
Washington, DC, Office:
      1710 Rhode Island Ave. NW, Suite 900, Washington, DC 20036-3132
Eugene, Oregon, Office:
      180 West 8th Ave., Suite 300, Eugene, OR 97401-2916
Order Desk: 1.800.336.5191
Order Fax: 1.541.302.3778
Customer Service: orders@iste.org
Book Publishing: books@iste.org
Book Sales and Marketing: booksmarketing@iste.org
Web: www.iste.org

**Cover Photos:** © iStockphoto.com/Edyta Pawlowska (*left*), © iStockphoto.com/Quavondo (*top right*), © Image Source/Corbis (*middle right*), © John Lund/Drew Kelly/Blend Images/Corbis (*bottom right*)

**Inside Photos:** © iStockphoto.com
Ch. 1, Brad Killer; Ch. 2, Catherine Yeulet; Ch. 3, Gary Sludden; Ch. 4, Dmitriy Filippov; Ch. 5, Kim Gunkel; Ch. 6, Muammer Mujdat Uzel; Ch. 7, Jacek Chabraszewski; Ch. 8, Avava; Ch. 9, Christopher Futcher; Ch. 10, Sean Locke; Ch. 11, Williv; Ch. 12, Monika Adamczyk; Tips, Robertas Narkus

# About ISTE

The International Society for Technology in Education (ISTE) is the trusted source for professional development, knowledge generation, advocacy, and leadership for innovation. ISTE is the premier membership association for educators and education leaders engaged in improving teaching and learning by advancing the effective use of technology in PK–12 and teacher education.

Home of the National Educational Technology Standards (NETS) and ISTE's annual conference and exposition (formerly known as NECC), ISTE represents more than 100,000 professionals worldwide. We support our members with information, networking opportunities, and guidance as they face the challenge of transforming education. To find out more about these and other ISTE initiatives, visit our website at **www.iste.org**.

As part of our mission, ISTE Book Publishing works with experienced educators to develop and produce practical resources for classroom teachers, teacher educators, technology leaders, and parents. Every manuscript we select for publication is carefully peer-reviewed and professionally edited. We look for content that emphasizes the effective use of technology where it can make a difference—both at school and at home. We value your feedback on this book and other ISTE products. E-mail us at **books@iste.org**.

# About the Author

**Holly Poteete** draws on more than 11 years of experience with elementary and middle schools across the country. In addition to her classroom experience, she has taught technology classes for educators and parents. The Georgia Department of Education has published many of her web-based lesson plans that integrate technology with core curriculum standards. Holly is the author of the first and second editions of *The Computer Lab Teacher's Survival Guide: K–6 Lessons for the Whole Year,* (2003, 2010). She believes in the importance of instilling in children the desire to master skills, so that they will continue to learn throughout their lives. Holly and her husband, Paul, are the parents of two children and reside in Monterey, California.

## Contributions

I want to thank my technology-savvy husband, Paul Poteete, who is a chief information security officer, for assisting me with this book. He has clarified many important Internet safety strategies that will help keep our children safe.

# Contents

## Chapter 3
# Keyboarding ...... **73**

## Chapter 4
# The World Wide Web ...... **97**

## Chapter 5
# Word Processing ....................................................... **123**

## Chapter 6
# Internet Research .................................................. **149**

## Chapter 9
# Multimedia Presentations

## Chapter 10
# Graphs and Spreadsheets

Chapter 11

# Inside a Computer ........... **283**

Chapter 12

# Web 2.0 Activities ........... **309**

# Appendixes

# Introduction

Children are using computers at increasingly early ages and through the Internet have access to an expanding amount of information. This book provides parents with the information they need to successfully teach their children, preschool through sixth grade, about numerous technical concepts while also providing parents with many hands-on activities to teach their children about important technology skills, everything from keyboarding to Internet safety.

Throughout my 11 years of experience in working with children in various schools throughout the United States, I have discovered some interesting ideas and have developed new approaches to technology instruction in the schools. Now, as a parent of two children, I realize the importance of instilling the knowledge of appropriate technology use early in our children, because sometimes schools are not teaching them everything they need to know about computer use. We are ultimately responsible for our children, and this book provides parents with a tool to use at home in a safe learning environment. Even if schools are teaching computer skills to your child, this book will fill in any gaps as well as show your children that you feel these concepts are important and worth learning. It is better to train them to do the right things the first time when they are young, instead of waiting until they are older and retraining them.

As a parent, you can use this book with minimal computer knowledge. You will need a computer with Internet access for many, but not all, of the activities. If you don't have a computer, you can still use many of the activities, and then go to the library or another place to use a computer when it is needed for the activity. If you don't have Internet access, you could do the activities that require online access at the library or another location that has a computer connected to the Internet.

This book provides step-by-step activities that you can do with your child based on ISTE's (International Society for Technology in Education) National Educational Standards for Students (NETS•S; see Appendix B). The CD that comes with this book includes more than 100 supplemental files, including multimedia presentations, worksheets, quizzes, learning cards, and other files used in the chapters.

The chapters in this book are a guide for your own ideas and concepts. Tap into your own personality and teaching style to enrich the chapters I have provided. Even more important than the curriculum in this book is the hidden curriculum, the manner in which the lessons are portrayed to your child. With the ideas in these activities and your own personal flair, you can empower children with technological information.

Your children will see your excitement and will experience technology as never before, as they engage in new and inspiring activities. Understanding technology has become a necessity in today's society, and children with a solid background in technology will have the foundation necessary to succeed in the future. This book gives parents with and without computer backgrounds the tools they need to effectively teach technology.

# Organization of This Book

The main section of this book is divided into 12 chapters. Each chapter has 10 activities that teach the chapter concepts in various ways, such as creating a book, performing Internet research, doing a website scavenger hunt, or watching a slide show. The activities have three to six steps for parents to follow as they teach their children. Each chapter provides many enrichment activities and suggestions for varying the activites based on age and learning styles. The chapters are meant to be taught in order, because some skills taught earlier are used in later chapters. The activities in each chapter are also intended to be taught in order, because some of the work completed in an activity may be used in a later activity. However, you can certainly modify the order of chapters and activities, if needed for your particular requirements. A chart summarizing the chapter objectives appears on the next page.

## Compact Disc

There is a CD located in the back of this book that includes all of the supplemental material for each chapter: worksheets, quizzes, answer keys, recording sheets, learning cards, and other learning materials. The CD supplements are listed in the Materials section of each activity. The files can be opened by Windows, Mac, and Linux computers and can be modified, if desired. Your child can type directly into the Word version of many worksheets and tests. Supplements in PDF format are also included on the CD for your convenience. The files on the CD are organized and named by chapter. To make locating and using these supplements faster and easier, it is recommended that you copy all files to your hard drive before beginning the lessons.

## Chapters and Chapter Objectives

| Chapter | Objective |
|---|---|
| **Chapter 1**<br>**Computer Basics** | Children will be able to summarize knowledge of 12 computer devices by doing one or more of the following: drawing the device, explaining the purpose of the device, describing the device, examining the device, or locating the actual device. |
| **Chapter 2**<br>**Safety on the Internet** | Children will learn about Internet safety and how to be good digital citizens when using the computer through many activities, using songs, stories, slide shows, games, and a contract. |
| **Chapter 3**<br>**Keyboarding** | Children will demonstrate the correct keyboarding and finger positions and type with increasing accuracy by participating in many different keyboarding activities. |
| **Chapter 4**<br>**The World Wide Web** | Children will learn about basic navigation on the World Wide Web, Internet infrastructure, URLs (Uniform Resource Locators), web browsers, IP (Internet Protocol) addresses, download speeds, switches, and hubs. |
| **Chapter 5**<br>**Word Processing** | Children will learn basic word processing skills using tutorials, worksheets, checklists, and a word processor. |
| **Chapter 6**<br>**Internet Research** | Children will learn to research on the Internet using a variety of methods and fun topics and then create a slide presentation using the information that they gathered during the research activities. |
| **Chapter 7**<br>**Peripheral Devices** | Children will research, identify, and describe 25 peripheral devices using a slide show, a scavenger hunt, books, games, research, and learning cards. |
| **Chapter 8**<br>**Communicating Using the Internet** | Children will learn the basics of how to communicate using e-mail (electronic mail), IM (instant messaging), VoIP (Voice over Internet Protocol), and videoconferencing using slide shows, worksheets, and learning cards, as well as actual hands-on Internet communication experiences. |
| **Chapter 9**<br>**Multimedia Presentations** | Children will be able to create and present a unique multimedia slide show by working through activities such as watching online stories and slide show tutorials, and using a storyboard to write and illustrate a story. |
| **Chapter 10**<br>**Graphs and Spreadsheets** | Children will produce several creative graphs using a computer spreadsheet application and learn many skills such as sorting and creating formulas. |
| **Chapter 11**<br>**Inside a Computer** | Children will be able to summarize knowledge of 18 computer parts by doing one or more of the following: drawing the part, explaining the purpose of the part, describing the part, examining the part, or locating the actual part. |
| **Chapter 12**<br>**Web 2.0 Activities** | Children will experience and learn the basics of several Web 2.0 concepts including blogs, podcasts, RSS (Really Simple Syndication) feeds, wikis, and video-sharing sites while practicing Internet safety. |

# How to Use This Book

This book can be used for several years with your children. The variety of activities offered in each chapter will keep your children interested as they learn important technology skills and concepts. When they are young, use the activities that are marked with the "Easy to Modify for Younger Kids" icon. As they grow older, you can reuse the book by using the suggested variations and the enrichment activities listed for each chapter. You can also repeat activities for a review using a different website, because several sites are listed for each activity. Keep this in mind, and as you complete activities, maintain a record of the websites you used and the activities that you did with your child.

This book includes 12 chapters with 10 activities in each chapter; therefore, there are 120 activities for your child to complete in this book. You should think about and plan out an instruction method that works for your child's schedule. Here are a few suggestions of schedules you can incorporate to teach technology to your child in your home.

Because there are 12 chapters, you could focus on one chapter a month and do two or three activities per week so that you will complete the entire book in one year. Since there will be 10 activities to complete in one month, your child could do an activity every Monday, Wednesday, and Friday and then repeat a favorite activity during the extra days on the last week of the month.

You could also do two chapters a month and complete the book in six months. If you choose this method, your child will have 20 activities to complete in one month and will need to complete at least one activity every weekday.

You may want Monday to be technology day, or maybe teach technology every Tuesday and Thursday, or maybe a certain month can be technology month. Most of the activities can be completed in 30 minutes; however, some could be completed over several days. You could even do one activity a week. Choose a time of day, morning, afternoon, or evening, that works best for instruction for you and your child.

If you teach other subjects to your child, use a monthly calendar to record the various subjects with tentative times. You can download yearly calendars using the Internet with the months and dates already filled in for you for the current year. You may even want to create a weekly or daily schedule for your child.

Be flexible. If you plan an activity to be completed in a certain time, but your child needs more time, allow your child to complete the activity instead of rushing to the next one just to meet a timeline. If you take the time to create a schedule now of how and when you plan on teaching technology to your child, then as you begin to use this book, you will have a sense of your child's overall learning goals for the future. If you do not need or want to create a schedule, that is okay, too. Just pick up the book, open it to an activity, and try it with your child.

## Plan

Review and prepare for the technology activity when you have a few minutes by yourself. Read through each lesson and make sure you are familiar with all the skills your child will need to learn. Try to have everything ready for the lesson before you begin. Print and review all of the CD supplements.

For each activity, write simple steps on a large piece of paper or board and allow your child to follow the steps so he knows what he is doing next. These steps will guide you as you instill these important technology concepts in your child. After you complete each step, place a checkmark next to it showing that it has been completed. This will help you and your child to stay focused on each step of the technology lesson, especially if there is an interruption and you must stop working in the middle of the lesson, which happens quite often to me at home. You may want to include any websites that you will be using so your child can type it into the address bar by himself. For younger children, you probably want to have the page already open, or just type it for them so they can watch how to open a webpage. It is okay if you don't finish everything you had planned on your list; just save it for another day.

## Lesson Plans

The table of contents can be used as a lesson-planning tool. Begin by writing the date that you plan on teaching each chapter next to the name of the chapter. This will give you an overall view of the dates you plan to use when teaching the book. You may choose not to assign a date for each activity at this time. It depends on how disciplined you wish to be when teaching your child and whether you would like to teach a certain activity at a certain time. As you begin teaching a chapter, you can write in the dates for each activity at that time. Remember to make notes in pencil— you will probably change the dates because things happen and schedules change. This is also a great place to record notes about activities that seemed to really help your child or to make a note of anything that you would like to repeat or change in future lessons.

## Grade Book and Activity Achievement Chart

Use the Grade Book provided in Appendix A at the back of this book, and also on the CD, to record the date and grade for each chapter and activity. If you have several children, print one Grade Book for each child. There is a place to record the date your child completed the activity and your child's grade for each activity. There is also a box to record the chapter average and grade. Below is a sample from the Grade Book.

Grade Book Sample

| Activities | Date | Grade |
|---|---|---|
| 1. Computer Basics Slide Show | | |
| 2. Online Research | | |
| 3. Identify the Devices | | |
| 4. Make a Book | | |
| 5. Website Scavenger Hunt | | |
| 6. Coloring Book | | |
| 7. Computer Device Cards | | |
| 8. Design a Computer System | | |
| 9. Slide Show Quiz | | |
| 10. Quiz | | |

Chapter Average: _____

Chapter Grade: _____

If you would like a way for your child to keep track of her achievements and progress in this book, then your child can use the Activity Achievement Chart, which is included on the CD. This chart provides a place for your child to record the date she completed the activity and her grade for each activity. Using this chart will allow her to keep track of her progress in completeing the activites and to show her achievements. Your child could place a sticker or checkmark next to each activity once it is completed. She could also circle or put a star next to the activities that she will be working on that day to help herself keep track of upcoming activities. Seeing the list of completed activities can provide your child with a sense of accomplishment. You may want to put the Activity Achievement Chart in a 3-ring notebook for your child, and have her keep all of the work completed from the activites in this notebook.

## Grades

There are many methods of providing feedback to your children in the form of grades. For younger children, you could draw a smiley face, or they could put a small sticker in the grade column next to each activity that they complete. You may decide to use E for Excellent, VG for Very Good, and so on. You could draw a checkmark, check-plus, and check-minus in the grade column to show your child's achievements. A check could mean the activity was completed, a check plus could mean they completed the activity and did exceptional work, and a check minus could mean to try harder next time. For older children, you could use some type of point system, such as every activity is worth 10 points and at the end of the chapter, you count up all of the points they received for each activity to assign them an overall chapter percentage. For example, if you awarded them 9 points on the first activity, and 7 points on the second activity, and 10 points on the remaining eight activities, their total points would be 96, so they would earn a 96% for the chapter. You may or may not decide to assign grades for their activities, but try to have some type of record of their work to show and remind them about their technological achievements using this book.

## Software

There are several chapters in the book that use word processing, spreadsheet, and multimedia presentation software. For your convenience, I have included instructions on how to use the products in the Microsoft Office suite (Word, Excel, and PowerPoint) as well as the products in the free OpenOffice.org open source office software suite (Writer, Calc, and Impress). If you plan on using the OpenOffice.org software, you will want to install it before starting the lessons. It can be downloaded from the OpenOffice.org website (www.openoffice.org). All three programs (plus the rest of the components in the suite) will be downloaded at the same time, so you don't need to download each program separately.

# Chapter Layout

The following paragraphs discuss the content and arrangement of the chapters and activities in greater detail. Each chapter includes the following sections: Objective, Purpose, Activities Overview, CD Supplements, Variations for Younger Children, Internet Safety, Fun Decorations, Vocabulary, NETS•S Addressed, Grades, Enrichment, Closure, and 10 learning activities. Each learning activity includes the following items: Goal, Materials, and Steps. Tips are offered for some activities.

## Objective

This section provides a simple statement of what children will learn by the end of the chapter.

## Purpose

Use the information in the Purpose category to inform your child about the specific skills she will have by the end of the lesson and to describe why the chapter is important. Convey to your child the significance of knowing about the content in each chapter, because she will work harder if she knows it will help her in the future.

## Activities Overview

This section lists all of the activities in the chapter and gives some ideas of how to effectively teach the activities to your child. Carefully consider which activities will benefit your children depending on their age, abilities, and learning styles. Some children may be able to complete all of the activites, while others would benefit by focusing more time on a few key activities. Certain children may require a more structured environment, whereas a self-motivated child could be given more freedom to work. Don't hurry to complete an activity just to have it completed; children should work at their own pace and really understand the concepts.

There is also a helpful chart that categorizes each activity using the following columns: Worksheet, Modifiable (to indicate that the activity is easily modifiable for younger children), Internet Access, Game, Learning Cards, Slide Show, Arts and Crafts, and Answer Key. This chart will help you to plan the lessons to best suit your child. For example, if you feel that your child would benefit from an arts and crafts activity at a

Sample Chapter Chart

| Activities | Worksheet | Modifiable* | Internet Access | Game | Learning Cards | Slide Show | Arts and Crafts | Answer Key |
|---|---|---|---|---|---|---|---|---|
| 1. Computer Basics Slide Show | | ✔ | | | | ✔ | | |
| 2. Online Research | ✔ | ✔ | | | | | | ✔ |
| 3. Identify the Devices | | ✔ | | ✔ | | | | |
| 4. Make a Book | | ✔ | | | | | ✔ | |
| 5. Website Scavenger Hunt | | | ✔ | ✔ | | | | |
| 6. Coloring Book | ✔ | ✔ | | | | | ✔ | |
| 7. Computer Device Cards | ✔ | | | | ✔ | | | |
| 8. Design a Computer System | | ✔ | | | | | ✔ | |
| 9. Slide Show Quiz | | | | | | ✔ | | ✔ |
| 10. Quiz | ✔ | ✔ | | | | | | ✔ |

* Easily modifiable for younger children

particular time, then choose an activity with a checkmark in the Arts and Crafts column. If access to the Internet is an issue, you can easily see which activities require Internet access. The figure above is a sample chart from Chapter 1: "Computer Basics."

## Activities and Learning Styles

The activities overview chart can also help you determine which activites will best support your child's learning style. The three main types of learning styles are visual, auditory, and tactile (kinesthetic). Visual learners learn best by seeing and looking. Auditory learners learn best by hearing and listening. Tactile or kinesthetic learners learn best by doing and touching. Most people learn using several learning styles, but there is probably one type that is predominant in your child. For example, if your child is mainly a visual learner, activites using the learning cards will be a good choice. If your child is mainly a tactile learner, activities involving arts and crafts or games would be a good choice. If your child is a visual and auditory learner, the slide shows will be a great learning tool.

## CD Supplements

Many of the activities use supplemental materials, which are worksheets (creative, fill-in-the-blank, matching, and multiple choice), slide shows, quizzes, recording sheets, learning cards, and other learning materials that help teach the concepts. This section lists the supplements used in the chapter, all of which can be found on the CD. It would be a good idea to review all of the supplements for each activity before beginning the lesson. You may wish to print all of the CD supplements and place them in a three-ring binder, making the documents easy to view and distribute to your child.

## Variations for Younger Children

Each chapter gives several suggestions for ways to make the activities more appropriate for younger children. Feel free to modify the activities, such as removing a step, to meet the needs of your child.

## Internet Safety

In all of the chapters, there are certain activities that require Internet access. Remember to think about the following Internet safety tips during these activities:

- Use web-filtering software, service, or an appliance when allowing access to the Internet, such as www.netnanny.com, www.cyberpatrol.com, or www.cybersitter.com.

- Monitor your child closely while using the Internet.

- Keep the computer in an open location such as a living room or kitchen.

- Communicate often with your child about his online communication with others.

- Clearly define your expectations of what to do and what not to do when using the computer in a way that your child understands.

- Remind your child to be a good digital citizen by behaving appropriately and ethically and only talking with people that he already knows.
- Monitor the computer's web browser "cache" and website history.

If you are concerned about your child's computer usage and are unable to concurrently observe his access, you might consider installing keylogging software on your computer. Keyloggers will record every keystroke that your child types on the keyboard and store the information in a text file, e-mail, or on an external device.

During the Internet activities, constantly monitor your child's progress. This is especially important when children are researching on the Internet. Remind your child that if a bad page pops up, she should immediately let you know so that you can close it. Even though your home may have a web filtering system, some advertisements may pop up that are inappropriate for children. If you notice inappropriate advertisements on websites meant for children, please notify the website owner. For more information and activities on Internet safety, refer to Chapter 2: "Safety on the Internet."

## Fun Decorations

This section provides several examples of possible room decorations that will inspire your child as well as focus his attention on the concepts being learned. Simple pictures can generate enthusiasm as well as provide another opportunity to teach your child about the information in the chapter. A few of the decorations listed are even used as part of the activities.

## Vocabulary

In each chapter there are specific terms that you will need to teach your child. These terms are listed here so that you can review them and have a basic understanding of the vocabulary. You can use the vocabulary worksheet for your child to write down the definitions to the vocabulary words in each chapter. The vocabulary worksheet is located on the CD and is the last CD supplement listed for each chapter.

## NETS•S Addressed

Each chapter is designed to address one or more of the National Educational Technology Standards for Students (NETS•S). These technology standards are a nationally recognized, specific list of concepts that your child should know concerning technology. Furthermore, there are standards for other subjects such as mathematics, language arts, social studies, science, physical education, dance, health, foreign language, art, and music. It may be beneficial for your children if you perform a search on certain national or state learning standards and see if they know the content for their grade levels.

The complete NETS•S are presented in Appendix B.

## Grades

This section lists several ways you can assess your child throughout the chapter. It is important to give feedback to your children that is accurate and shows what they learned. You may want to use the Grade Book to record their grades and achievements. This is located as an appendix in the back of this book and also on the CD.

## Enrichment

The Enrichment section provides activity ideas for children who need a more challenging learning activity or just another way to reinforce the content in the chapter. You could also think of your own activities to encourage excellence in your child.

## Closure

This section sums up the lesson in a few words and offers concluding remarks and a few simple activities. Closure activities give children an opportunity to reflect on what they have learned and to reinforce the knowledge they have gained.

## Ten Learning Activities

The 10 learning activities in each chapter have simple titles that describe the activity, such as Internet Safety Song, Make a Book, or Slide Show Quiz. In order to meet the needs of children within their various learning styles and personalities, the 10 activities in each chapter teach the information in different ways, such as singing a song, researching online, taking a quiz, or playing a game. It also keeps your children focused on one concept using different learning methods. Take note of which activities your children seem to like best, and use this information when teaching them in the future. The following items are included in each activity: Goal, Materials, and Steps. Tips are offered for some activities.

### Goal

The goal is a simple statement of what your child should be able to do by the end of the activity.

### Materials

A detailed list of the items needed to teach the activity is given here. Optional materials are also included. This section also lists all the associated files, called "supplements," for the activity. These supplements are provided on the accompanying CD.

### Steps

Each activity has three to six steps to teach the concept. The steps can be used as a guide; feel free to modify the steps to meet your individual needs. The activities in each chapter are intended to be taught in order because some of the work completed in the activity may be used in a later activity. In some of the activities children work mostly independently, whereas in others the parent works together with the child to show the child a concept.

### Tips

At the end of most activities there is a tip box that suggests things to consider, such as different things you can try and some ways you can modify the activity or change it.

# How Can I Successfully Teach Technology to My Child?

You can most successfully teach technology by being yourself. Cultivate a positive learning environment that inspires your child to reach beyond ordinary methods of learning. Your child will be motivated by your enthusiastic attitude toward technology and willingness to learn new concepts. The activities in this book are easy to follow and modify for your particular needs. Technology has changed the way we live and will continue to revolutionize our world. Children easily adapt to innovations in technology and revolutionary ideas in education. Because children have no fear when deciphering a computer issue or solving a technical problem, a variety of new activities can and should be incorporated into their lives to teach technological concepts.

This book will benefit parents who would like to teach an intense technology curriculum with their child as well as parents who would like to use this book in a more relaxed manner. Whatever the goal or technique, know that you will be teaching important technology skills that children can use for school subjects and life experiences during your instruction. Time goes by fast as we raise our children. Take a few moments to reinforce important technology concepts with your child at opportune times. You are creating a technological foundation for your child every day. Remember to use the NETS•S, which provide specific outcomes for childrens' abilities in technology, as your guide. Your excitement and new ideas will inspire your children to become highly technologically literate lifelong learners.

## Teachable Moments

Take advantage of those teachable moments when your child asks you a question or something happens in your life that could be a real technological learning experience for your child. For example, one day a terrible windstorm caused us to lose power at our home for about a week. We decided to purchase a generator to get power. We explained to our young son that the generator supplies electricity and gives us the ability to use the refrigerator, lights, and computers. There are also times when we are out shopping and I see a certain device, such as an iPod or a keyboard. I sometimes take advantage of these times and talk about the device and what it does to help us. Computers surround us in many aspects of our lives. Learning more about them will help your child in all areas of life.

## Atmosphere

Atmosphere is an integral part of a successful computer activity. When your child begins to work, he should see and feel structure during the activity. Appearances matter. The room should be cleaned regularly and trash should be kept off the floor to the best of your ability. Also, the table, monitor, and tower or laptop should be dusted and cleaned frequently. If you show respect for the workspace, so will your child. If possible, the computer wires and cables should be out of sight. There are many ways to cover and hide the cables—for example, drop boxes, corrugated tubing, cable ties, Velcro ties, or self-adhesive cord holders, just to name a few. An organized workspace reduces distractions that may compete for your child's attention.

If you have a specific room in which to teach your child, or even if you have a specific area of your home, you could decorate it in a fun way. Decide on a fun theme for your computer area, such as frogs, rainforests, the ocean, farm animals, or anything else of interest. Go to a fabric or discount store to buy cheerful colored fabric displaying the theme and hang it up to create a section of your wall to use as a bulletin board. The fabric may also be used as a tablecloth for the printer table or other surface. Decorate the room with several objects related to the theme hanging from the ceiling. You could even place a fun carpet in a special location in the room. You could go online and search for decorations to use in this area.

If you have a computer projector, you could connect it to your computer to project information onto a screen or a blank wall to show the slide shows or even teach a certain activity for added fun.

## Management

If you are teaching two children at the same time with two computers, one computer management technique is to create something that can attach to the side or top of the monitor to let you know that your child has a question. Here is an example of how to use a Popsicle stick to create a sign for your child to turn when they have a question.

Cut out a green and a red circle using construction paper. Each circle should be the same size. Glue the circles on top of each other to one end of a large Popsicle stick, so you can see a red circle on one side and a green circle on the other side. Attach a small Velcro square to each side of the other end of the Popsicle stick. Attach a small Velcro square to the side or top of the monitor.

When your child is working, keep the green circle facing her. When you child needs help, have her switch the popsicle stick to the red circle so you know that she needs help.

When your child has a question, she turns the popsicle stick on the monitor to alert you but keeps working if you are busy. When using this method, you may find that by the time you get the opportunity to help, your child has been able to figure out the answer on her own.

Come up with a standard method of getting your child's attention quickly. This signal could be clapping in a special rhythm, ringing a bell, raising your hand, or anything else that could quickly and easily get your child to focus on you. Make a rule that while you are explaining a concept, your child is not allowed to work on the computer. Have your child sit with his hands folded so he is not tempted to type. Keep a box filled with small prizes. When your child completes an activity, allow him to choose a prize. Keep a pencil and some paper readily available next to the computer because many of the lessons require some writing. Following these guidelines when designing your computer area will create a fun atmosphere in which to learn technology.

## Ergonomics for Kids

In today's society, a growing number of children are using computers at home and at school for long periods of time. With the increased use of computers comes a higher risk of injury, including neck pain, back pain, and carpal tunnel syndrome. Designing a safe and healthy computing environment as well as developing correct posture strategies will educate children on this important issue.

Think about the best solution for your house to promote health and wellness for your children. The specific hardware devices as well as the arrangement of the computer should be carefully studied to determine whether any changes should be made to best meet the needs of your children. There are some inexpensive strategies you can implement to make the computer area appropriate for children.

Teach children at an early age the correct way to sit at the keyboard and the proper arrangement of the workstation to meet their comfort level. It is also important to teach children the reason for sitting with the correct posture and ensuring that the workstation meets their individual needs. If children understand that developing bad habits may cause them injuries that will prevent them from playing sports or using the computer for a while, they will probably listen and try to follow the guidelines you discuss. Talk to your children about how it would make them feel if they were unable to play baseball or use the games on the computer for six months. Try to get your child to understand the importance of correct posture and the proper arrangement of the computer workstation.

The following lists provide guidelines and suggestions for ensuring the safe use of computers in your home. Instruct your children to be aware of their position when using the computer, and arrange the room to meet their needs.

### Monitor

Dim the lights and close the blinds or curtains to minimize the glare on monitors so that children do not have to strain to see the computer screen. If the lights are dimmed, make sure your children can read any documents without straining their eyes. Arrange the computer so that the monitor does not face the windows, which also minimizes the glare.

Depending upon the size of the monitor, arrange the monitor so that it is far enough away from your child. The text or upper portion of the screen should be at eye level so children are not straining their necks to see the screen. The monitor can be slightly adjusted up and down for different heights.

Use lamps or free-standing miniature lights if your child needs to read or write while using the computer.

### Keyboard and Mouse

Buy wrists pads or make your own by rolling up a small cloth. Acquire small keyboards and mice for younger children. Children with small hands will be better able to reach the keys on a smaller keyboard and to move a smaller mouse.

Ensure that the mouse is easily reachable. If your children are not using the keyboard, it could be moved to the side and the mouse moved to the center so that the mouse is closer to them while working.

If keyboard legs are available, adjust them so that children are most comfortable when typing. Ensure that your children's arms are parallel to the keyboard and elbows are by their sides. If a taller chair is not available, your children could sit on a chair pad or foam so their arms are straight and parallel to the keyboard. Make sure that children are using the proper keyboarding position. The correct position is discussed in Chapter 3: "Keyboarding." Here are some things to remember:

- Eyes on monitor
- Wrists flat
- Fingers curved
- Feet flat on floor
- Back straight
- Fingers on home row

Ensure that children are sitting comfortably in the correct keyboarding position. While children are working, their shoulders should be relaxed. Have children use a document holder so that they do not have to strain their necks when looking at a document.

## Chair

Have children sit with their backs straight. If the chairs are curved or bent, a back pillow or foam could be used on the back of the chair so that your child can rest against the back of the chair while typing. Direct children to sit with their feet on the floor. If a child cannot reach the floor, a footstool or old phone books could be used so that he can rest his feet. Ensure that children can easily view text on the screen without bending their necks. Children could sit on foam pads or something similar so their eyes can see the top portion of the monitor.

## Breaks

While they are working, encourage children to take frequent stretch breaks. Teach simple exercises to your children, such as raising arms, opening and closing hands, touching toes, and reaching for the sky. Complete these when your children are sitting at the computer and working for long periods of time.

You could even make up a song so that children will remember to stretch when using the computer.

### Laptops

If using a laptop as your primary computer, you may need to use an external keyboard and mouse to ensure that your child's neck and arms are in the correct keyboarding position. You may also need to elevate the laptop to make sure the screen is at eye level.

If children understand the importance of sitting correctly and arranging the workstation appropriately at home, they will be more aware of these concerns when using the computer at school or the library.

# Internet Security

From anti-virus to encryption, there are many ways to secure the information on computers. Children should be able to be creative and explore technology in a safe digital environment. It is a delicate balance of allowing children to use technology while protecting them from the dangers that go along with online learning. Because each computer has different equipment and technologies, here are a few general ideas and simple steps to consider when determining if your computer is secure.

Perform a quick security assessment of your computer. Consider the time is would take for a hacker to access private information. Think about any vulnerable areas that could be compromised. Decide what level of security you want for the computer.

Secure private information on the computer. You could use encryption for certain drives to protect sensitive information if the drive or system is lost or stolen. Protect computers from viruses and malicious hacker attacks. Keep a backup of your data.

Create a technology security plan. Use web-filtering software or an appliance when allowing children to access the Internet. Install a firewall and anti-virus and anti-spyware software. Create logins and unbreakable passwords. Laptops with sensitive information that have wireless Internet access should have encrypted drives.

There are many ways to secure your computer and home network, so you may want to work with a computer security consultant to determine the best security options to best protect your children and the information on your computer. In many cases, your computer will not contain sensitive information. In those cases regular updates, good anti-virus software, and the operating system's built-in firewall will provide ample protection.

*I sincerely hope that you find the information in this book helpful in raising your digital child. Have fun learning about technology!  ~Holly Poteete*

## Chapter 1

# Computer Basics

## Objective

Children will be able to summarize knowledge of 12 computer devices by doing one or more of the following: drawing the device, explaining the purpose of the device, describing the device, examining the device, or locating the actual device.

## Purpose

Convey to your child the significance of knowing the basic computer devices. Your child will work harder to learn this information if she knows it will help her in the future. Explain that it is important to know the name and function of basic computer devices to successfully operate computers. Think of a unique way to provide reasons for learning so your child will be able to personally apply this information to her life.

# Activities Overview

This foundational chapter will help your child identify and understand basic computer devices and their uses. It provides the foundation and terminology to discuss and understand the rudiments of computers, and promotes the accurate use of computer devices. Children will employ critical-thinking skills while conducting research. They will summarize knowledge of 12 devices by doing one or more of the following: drawing the device, explaining the purpose of the device, describing the device, examining the device, or locating the actual device in the room.

To get started, you may plan a fun activity to focus your child's attention on technology. Be energetic while turning your child's attention to computers. Motivate your child by actively involving him in the activities.

The following chart lists and categorizes each activity to help you to plan the lessons. For example, if you feel that your child would benefit from a hands-on activity at a particular time, then choose an activity with a checkmark in the arts and crafts column.

| Activities | Worksheet | Modifiable* | Internet Access | Game | Learning Cards | Slide Show | Arts and Crafts | Answer Key |
|---|---|---|---|---|---|---|---|---|
| 1. Computer Basics Slide Show | | ✔ | | | | ✔ | | |
| 2. Online Research | ✔ | | ✔ | | | | | ✔ |
| 3. Identify the Devices | | ✔ | | ✔ | | | | |
| 4. Make a Book | | ✔ | | | | | ✔ | |
| 5. Website Scavenger Hunt | | | ✔ | ✔ | | | | |
| 6. Coloring Book | ✔ | ✔ | | | | | ✔ | |
| 7. Computer Device Cards | ✔ | | | | ✔ | | | |
| 8. Design a Computer System | | ✔ | | | | | ✔ | |
| 9. Slide Show Quiz | | | | | | ✔ | | ✔ |
| 10. Quiz | ✔ | ✔ | | | | | | ✔ |

* Easily modifiable for younger children

# CD Supplements

The following chart lists all of the CD supplements for this chapter and provides the CD filename, supplement title, and activity number. To make locating and using these supplements faster and easier, it is recommended that you copy all files to your hard drive before beginning the lessons.

| CD Filename | Title | Activity |
|---|---|---|
| 1A | Computer Basics Slide Show | 1 |
| 1B | Computer Basics Worksheet I | 2 |
| 1C | Computer Basics Worksheet II | 2 |
| 1D | Computer Basics Worksheet I Answers | 2 |
| 1E | Computer Basics Worksheet II Answers | 2 |
| 1F | Computer Basics Coloring Book | 6 |
| 1G | Computer Device Cards | 7 |
| 1H | Computer Basics Slide Show Quiz | 9 |
| 1I | Computer Basics Slide Show Quiz Answers | 9 |
| 1J | Computer Basics Quiz I | 10 |
| 1K | Computer Basics Quiz II | 10 |
| 1L | Computer Basics Quiz III | 10 |
| 1M | Computer Basics Quiz I Answers | 10 |
| 1N | Computer Basics Quiz II Answers | 10 |
| 1O | Computer Basics Quiz III Answers | 10 |
| 1P | Computer Basics Vocabulary | Optional |

## Variations for Younger Children

Younger children learn differently and are motivated to explore concepts by different factors. Provide younger children with several opportunities to learn the computer devices, taking into account their various learning styles. Feel free to modify the activities, such as removing a step, to meet the needs of your child. You could even make up your own activities. The following ideas may help.

- Concentrate on fewer computer devices throughout the chapter

- Use one website consistently when viewing the devices online.

- Have children participate in more hands-on experiences by encouraging them to examine the computer devices.

- Use a puppet to explain various computer devices.

- Make up a song to a popular nursery tune that incorporates the various computer devices. Sing this song with your child while pointing to the devices to aid in learning.

- Make up stories by giving the computer devices lifelike attributes to describe their purpose. Then discuss the relationships between the parts and the way they all need to work together, like a family, to make the computer function correctly.

## Internet Safety

In this chapter, some activities require Internet access. Remind your child to think about Internet safety during these activities. You may want to review the Internet safety tips listed on pages 10–11.

## Fun Decorations

An inspiring room atmosphere and decorated walls will excite your child and focus their attention on technology. Be inventive as you plan the room decorations, and remember to have fun! The following are some ideas that might help you with decorations.

- Print each page of the Computer Basics Slide Show (CD Supplement 1A), glue the words and pictures to construction paper, and then hang them on a wall or door.

- Print out and glue several of the Computer Device Cards (CD Supplement 1G) to large cloud shapes (cut out from blue or white construction paper) and hang them from the ceiling. You will also be able to use these cards for Activity 7: Computer Device Cards.

- Dedicate a section of your house to learning the computer devices. Refer to the information located in that area of your home throughout this chapter. Use a banner or letter cutouts to spell out "Computer Basics," the topic of this chapter. Hang completed Computer Basics work in this area.

- Change the screensaver or the desktop background of your computer to a picture of a computer part presented in this chapter.

## Vocabulary

Review the following terms with your child so that he or she can have a basic understanding of the vocabulary used in this chapter. You could also have your child write the definitions in the Computer Basics Vocabulary worksheet (CD Supplement 1P).

**cables:** Wires used to carry electricity.

**CD/DVD drive:** The device that reads information from the CD (compact disc) or DVD (digital video disc).

**CD/DVD:** Small optical disc on which data such as music, text, graphics, or video and audio files is digitally encoded.

**keyboard:** A hardware device consisting of buttons (keys) that the user presses to type characters into a computer.

**laptop:** A portable computer small enough to use on one's lap.

**monitor:** A video screen that takes signals from a computer and displays the information.

**mouse:** A hand-operated data input device that moves the cursor on a computer screen.

**mouse pad:** A flat pad designed to provide an optimum surface on which to use a mouse.

**printer:** A device that prints text or graphics on paper.

**speakers:** Electronic equipment used to play sound.

**tower:** A style of computer system in which components are arranged in a tall, narrow cabinet.

**USB drive:** A small storage device that plugs into a computer's USB (Universal Serial Bus) port.

# NETS•S Addressed

6. **Technology Operations and Concepts**

   Students demonstrate a sound understanding of technology concepts, systems, and operations. Students:

   a. understand and use technology systems

   b. select and use applications effectively and productively

   c. troubleshoot systems and applications

   d. transfer current knowledge to the learning of new technologies

# Grades

Think of the best way to determine your child's comprehension of the computer devices for each activity. Throughout each activity, evaluate your child while she works. When deciding on the type of assessment, consider her age and abilities. The following are some suggestions that might help you to assess your child.

- Use the answer key CD supplements in the various activities to grade the completed worksheets. Base the grades on accuracy or completion. You may want to use the Grade Book located in Appendix A at the back of this book to record her assignments and grades.

- Keep a running record of your child's progress to determine her comprehension and understanding of the content. Record these observations on paper or in the Grade Book (Appendix A).

- Ask your child to write down the definitions to the vocabulary words in this chapter using the Computer Basics Vocabulary worksheet (CD Supplement 1P). Observe your child as she is researching the computer devices on the Internet, and document her efforts.

# Enrichment

Learning takes place all of the time, so motivate your child to learn more about the computer devices on his own. The excitement of learning computer basics will probably motivate your child to learn more about technology. Children could become actively involved by deciding for themselves which enrichment activity to complete. You could plan additional ways to expand your children's minds and their comprehension of computers. Be creative in thinking of an advanced assignment for high achievers. Choose one of these extended activities, or come up with your own ideas to encourage your child to go beyond all that he has learned in this chapter.

- Direct your child to invent and design a futuristic computer that will help society. Have her draw a diagram and write a paragraph describing the purpose of this computer. Instruct your child to make a poster board using two of the computer devices and describe the way the two devices are dependent on each other.

- Have your child research and discuss different aspects and interesting facts regarding the computer devices, including drives in a computer (CD, DVD, USB), types of compact discs (CD-ROM, CD-R, CD-RW, DVD, DVD-R), and styles of printers (inkjet, laser, thermal, wax; color or black and white).

- Have your child research the various styles of each computer device used in the chapter, such as ergonomic keyboards and LCD monitors. Have your child draw a picture of an entire computer system, utilizing all the computer devices discussed in the chapter. Then ask him to write a paragraph explaining the purpose of each computer device and the way they interrelate.

- Direct your child to use the Internet to locate more computer devices that are not on the worksheet. Then she could illustrate and write a sentence describing the device and explain it to you.

## Closure

After all chapter activities have been completed, give your child a few minutes to reflect on all he has learned. Closure is an important part of the learning process because it gives children the opportunity to make the information their own. Take a few moments to congratulate your child on his accomplishments in learning the computer basics.

Encourage your child to share a few interesting facts or trivia he learned about computer devices. Have your child talk about an interesting technological device used at home and describe the way it helps your family. Encourage your child to share a concept that he has learned and the ways it will assist him in the future. Ask your child, "What have you learned about computer basics?"

Activity **1**

Easy to
Modify for
Younger Kids

# Computer Basics Slide Show

## Goal

Your child will recite the computer devices using a slide show presentation.

## Materials

- Computer Basics Slide Show (CD Supplement 1A)
- computer

## Steps

### 1. Prepare

Open the Computer Basics Slide Show (CD Supplement 1A).
Click on Slide Show > View Slide Show when you are ready to begin.

### 2. Assess

As your child watches the slide show, have him name any of the computer devices that he already knows. The slide show first shows a picture of the computer device, then the name of the computer device. This is a great way to assess what your child already knows about the computer devices in this chapter. You may be surprised!

### 3. Recite

Play the slide show again and have your child recite the computer devices as they appear on the screen. Tell your child to repeat after you if he needs help saying the name of the device. Replay the slide show a few times (if needed) to teach your child to correctly recite the names of all these parts.

**Tips**
During the presentation, discuss the difference between output and input devices. Add something new and interesting to the presentation such as music, animation, or various slide backgrounds.

Activity 2

# Online Research

## Goal

Your child will research computer devices on a website, and then draw an illustration of each computer device and write the purpose of the device in the boxes provided on a worksheet.

## Materials

- Computer Basics Worksheet I or II (CD Supplement 1B or 1C)
- Computer Basics Worksheet I or II Answers (CD Supplement 1D or 1E)
- pencil
- computer with Internet access

## Steps

### 1. Prepare

The following are several websites that could be used to find the computer devices. Become familiar with the websites ahead of time so that you can decide which sites will best meet the abilities of your child.

**How Stuff Works:** http://howstuffworks.com/pc.htm  –and–
   http://computer.howstuffworks.com/computer-peripherals-channel.htm.
   **Note:** Use the How Stuff Works search engine.

**Introduction to Computers:**
   www.grassrootsdesign.com/intro/hardware.php

**Jan's Illustrated Computer Literacy 101:**
   www.jegsworks.com/Lessons/lesson3/lesson3-1.htm

**Kids Domain Computer Connections: Computers Inside and Out:**
   www.kidsdomain.com/brain/computer/lesson/comp_les1.html

**TekMom's Technology Buzzwords for Students:**
   www.tekmom.com/buzzwords/#SearchBox

## 2. Teach

Show your child how to navigate the website and ways to locate the pictures and the purposes of the computer devices. You may want to locate one of the devices together with your child.

## 3. Worksheets

Decide which Computer Basics Worksheet (I or II) will best meet the needs of your child. Print the worksheet then ask your child to complete it.

If you are using Computer Basics Worksheet I (CD Supplement 1B), have your child locate the computer device on a website, and then draw an illustration of the computer device in the box provided.

You may need to help your child locate the devices. It may be fun to read some of the information on the sites while discussing the devices together. Strive to focus on the computer devices that seem to interest your child.

If you are using Computer Basics Worksheet II (CD Supplement 1C), ask your child to locate the computer device on a website, then draw an illustration and write the purpose of the computer device in the boxes provided. Have your child write the purpose of the device using her own words.

Your child should incorporate critical thinking skills when determining the purpose of each device. Your child should be excited to begin this Internet activity. Provide encouragement and support to help her discover information on her own.

## 4. Check

Use the Computer Basics Worksheet I or II Answers (CD Supplement 1D or 1E) to check your child's work.

Activity 3

# Identify the Devices

Easy to
Modify for
Younger Kids

## Goal

Your child will locate and identify computer devices.

## Materials

*   12 computer items (use as many as you have): cables, CD/DVD drive, CD and DVD, keyboard, laptop, monitor, mouse, mouse pad, printer, speakers, tower, and USB drive

## Steps

### 1. Prepare

Place the 12 computer items on a table, or a specific location in a room. Use as many actual devices as possible to give your child the opportunity to see the physical device. You could use a picture to represent the devices that you were unable to obtain for this activity.

### 2. Locate

Ask, "Can you find the speakers?" Commend your child after he locates the speakers. If he is unable to locate the speakers on the table, give a hint to help him locate them. For example, say, "This is the device that plays sound."

### 3. Examine

Continue this game with the other devices. After locating the device, allow your child to look at it and examine it closely. Discuss any interesting details about the devices.

### 4. Repeat

Repeat this activity, asking more specific questions or the purpose of the device such as, "Can you find the device that reads information from a compact disc?" If your child is unable to locate the CD/DVD drive on the table, give another hint to help him find it.

Activity **4**

# Make a Book

Easy to
Modify for
Younger Kids

## Goal

Your child will make a book on computer devices.

## Materials

- paper (any size or style)
- pencil
- crayons, markers, or colored pencils
- stickers (optional)
- stapler
- construction paper (optional)

## Steps

### 1. Draw

Ask your child to draw an illustration of one of the computer devices on a piece of blank paper while looking at the actual device or a picture of the device.

### 2. Label

Have your child write the name of the device on the paper. Allow her to be creative and write it anywhere on the paper.

### 3. Purpose

Ask your child to write the purpose of the device, describing what it does. Repeat steps 1–3 for each device.

### 4. Decorate

Allow your child to decorate each page using markers, colored pencils, or stickers. Your child could make a cover for the book from construction paper. Staple the pages together to make a book.

## 5. Read

Allow your child to read the book to you or someone else.

**Tip**
Allow your child to cut out pictures of these computer devices from old magazines or catalogs and glue them to the specific page of that device in her book.

Activity **5**

# Website Scavenger Hunt

## Goal

Your child will search for certain devices, pictures, or facts on websites.

## Materials

- computer with Internet Access
- paper and pencil

## Steps

### 1. Prepare

Choose a website and make a list of certain devices, pictures, or facts that you would like your child to find on that site. You could use some devices that your child needs to practice or choose new computer devices that you would like to teach.

**How Stuff Works:** www.howstuffworks.com/pc.htm  —and—
   http://computer.howstuffworks.com/computer-peripherals-channel.htm
**Note:** Use the How Stuff Works search engine

**Introduction to Computers:**
   www.grassrootsdesign.com/intro/hardware.php

**Jan's Illustrated Computer Literacy 101:**
   www.jegsworks.com/Lessons/lesson3/lesson3-1.htm

**Kids Domain Computer Connections: Computers Inside & Out:**
   www.kidsdomain.com/brain/computer/lesson/comp_les1.html

**TekMom's Technology Buzzwords for Students:**
   www.tekmom.com/buzzwords/#SearchBox

### 2. Directions

Explain to your child that he should look for a particular word, such as "monitor," or a picture, such as a picture of a mouse, or a certain fact, such as the purpose of a printer, on the website. Depending on the age of your child, you may need to help him navigate the site.

## 3. Search

Have your child open the site and begin searching for the items on your list. Have him make a check mark next to the item on the paper when it is located on the site.

**Tips**
Time your child for each item to find out which items were the quickest to locate and which ones were more difficult. Create a fill-in-the-blank worksheet for your child by writing a sentence from a website leaving one word out. Your child must search for the missing word.

Activity **6**

Easy to
Modify for
Younger Kids

# Coloring Book

## Goal

Your child will color a coloring book on the computer devices.

## Materials

- Computer Basics Coloring Book (CD Supplement 1F), printed in black and white
- computer with Internet access
- crayons, markers, or colored pencils

## Steps

### 1. Websites

Choose a website from Activity 5 to show your child pictures and information about the computer devices.

### 2. Color

Allow your child to use crayons, markers, or colored pencils to color the computer devices in the Computer Basics Coloring Book (CD Supplement 1F) as you read about them on the website.

### 3. Discover

Your child may want to explore some of the other devices on the screen. Give her an opportunity to explore with your guidance.

**Tips**
For fun, allow your child to make her own book by stapling the coloring book pages together. She could use glitter or stickers to decorate the cover of the book.

Activity 7

# Computer Device Cards

## Goal

Your child will identify computer devices by labeling them with the Computer Device Cards.

## Materials

- Computer Device Cards (CD Supplement 1G)
- scissors, tape
- 12 computer items (use as many as you have): cables, CD/DVD drive, CD and DVD, keyboard, laptop, monitor, mouse, mouse pad, printer, speakers, tower, and USB drive

## Steps

### 1. Prepare

Print and then cut out the Computer Device Cards (CD Supplement 1G).

### 2. Discuss

As you show each card, give your child an opportunity to tell you about the computer device and explain the purpose of the computer device to you. If your child is still learning to read, just read the card for him, and then allow him to share. You could also describe the function of a particular computer device, and then your child could find the corresponding card.

### 3. Label

Have your child label the computer parts in your room with the device cards using tape. If you don't have some of the computer devices, just allow your child to explain what it looks like or what it does.

## 4. Check

Check each card to see if your child put the card in the correct place. If your child needs extra practice, do the activity again.

**Tips**
Try to have your child memorize the various computer devices. If you show your enthusiasm and interest while teaching, your child will catch the excitement to learn. Think of a way to instruct your child and bring him to the next level in his understanding of technology.

Activity 8

# Design a Computer System

Easy to
Modify for
Younger Kids

## Goal

Your child will plan and design an ideal computer system using pictures.

## Materials

- paper
- pictures of computer parts (from magazines or catalogs)
- scissors
- glue
- crayons, markers, or colored pencils

## Steps

### 1. Prepare

Talk to your child about her ideal or perfect computer system. Ask, "What would you like to have on your dream computer?" Your child can begin brainstorming and writing on a piece of paper any ideas about what her ideal computer would include, such as a wireless mouse, a built-in camera, an ergonomic keyboard, tiny speakers, CD/DVD drive, large monitor, or anything else. She can use devices learned in the chapter as well as other computer parts and accessories to design her computer.

### 2. Magazines

From old magazines or catalogs, have your child cut out pictures of computer parts that she wants to use for her ideal computer system.

### 3. Glue

Next, instruct your child to glue the pictures to a piece of paper to create her ideal system. If she was unable to find a picture of something, she could draw it using crayons, markers, or colored pencils.

## 4. Display

Have your child share her computer system with you and explain the different parts she included with her computer. Display her paper in your home.

Activity 9

# Slide Show Quiz

## Goal

Your child will take a slide show quiz on the computer devices.

## Materials

- Computer Basics Slide Show Quiz (CD Supplement 1H)
- Computer Basics Slide Show Quiz Answers (CD Supplement 1I)
- computer
- paper and pencil

## Steps

### 1. Prepare

Open the Computer Basics Slide Show Quiz (CD Supplement 1H). Click Slide Show > View Slide Show when you are ready to begin.

### 2. Write

Have your child write the answers on a piece of paper during the slide show. Your child could advance the slide show throughout the presentation. He will enjoy helping with the slide show, and this could aid in the learning process.

### 3. Check

Use the Computer Basics Slide Show Quiz Answers (CD Supplement 1I) to go over the answers to the slide show quiz.

Activity **10**

# *Quiz*

## Goal

Your child will take a computer basics quiz.

## Materials

- Computer Basics Quiz I, II, or III (CD Supplement 1J, 1K, or 1L)
- Computer Basics Quiz I, II, or III Answers (CD Supplement 1M, 1N, or 1O)
- computer or pencil

## Steps

### 1. Prepare

Decide which Computer Basics Quiz (I, II, or III) will best meet the needs of your child. Print the appropriate quiz (CD Supplement 1J, 1K, or 1L).

### 2. Quiz

Explain the instructions at the top of the assessment. Go over any questions. Give your child enough time to take the quiz to determine all that she has learned about computers during this chapter.

### 3. Check

Use the Computer Basics Quiz I, II, or III Answers (CD Supplement 1M, 1N, or 1O) to grade your child's work. Go over any missed questions with your child.

## Chapter 2

# Safety on the Internet

## Objective

Children will learn about Internet safety and how to be good digital citizens when using the computer through many activities, using songs, stories, slide shows, games, and a contract.

## Purpose

When surfing the World Wide Web, every click is potentially dangerous. Explain to your children that the Internet is fun, but they should be cautious when online. Instill in them that it is for their protection to use technology safely and practice ethical behavior when using a computer. Emphasize the importance of knowing safe behavior and proper etiquette when using the Internet to become good digital citizens.

## Activities Overview

The Internet safety and netiquette activities in this chapter offer a solid foundation for using the Internet safely and considerately. Carefully consider which activities and websites will benefit your child depending on his or her age, abilities, and learning styles. Some children may be able to complete all of the activities, while others would benefit by focusing more time on a few key activities.

At the completion of this chapter, your child should have a sound understanding of ways to stay safe on the Internet and ways to be polite when working online. Encourage your children as they work; they will be able to do a lot more if they feel that you believe in them.

Remember, don't hurry to complete an activity just to have it completed; your child should work at her own pace and really understand the concepts. To get started, you may decide to plan a fun activity to inspire your child and focus attention on Internet safety. A lively event will prompt children to focus on Internet safety, and they will be more interested and ready to learn.

| Activities | Worksheet | Modifiable* | Internet Access | Game | Learning Cards | Slide Show | Arts and Crafts | Answer Key |
|---|---|---|---|---|---|---|---|---|
| 1. Internet Safety Song | | ✔ | ✔ | | | ✔ | ✔ | |
| 2. Online Interactive Stories | | ✔ | ✔ | | | | | |
| 3. Golden Rule | | ✔ | | | | | ✔ | |
| 4. Internet Safety Terms | ✔ | | ✔ | | | | | |
| 5. Internet Safety Slide Show | | ✔ | | | | ✔ | | |
| 6. Treasure Hunt Game | | | | ✔ | ✔ | | | |
| 7. Internet Safety Games | | ✔ | ✔ | ✔ | | | | |
| 8. Contract | ✔ | ✔ | | | | | | |
| 9. Netiquette | | | | | | | ✔ | |
| 10. Quiz | ✔ | | | | | | | ✔ |

* Easily modifiable for younger children

# CD Supplements

The following chart lists all of the CD supplements for this chapter and provides the CD filename, supplement title, and activity number. To make locating and using these supplements faster and easier, it is recommended that you copy all files to your hard drive before beginning the lessons.

| CD Filename | Title | Activity |
|---|---|---|
| 2A | SafeKids Online Song Lyrics Slide Show | 1 |
| 2B | Internet Safety Terms Worksheet | 4 |
| 2C | Internet Safety Slide Show | 5 |
| 2D | Internet Safety Cards | 6 |
| 2E | Internet Safety Contract | 8 |
| 2F | Internet Safety Quiz | 10 |
| 2G | Internet Safety Quiz Answers | 10 |
| 2H | Safety on the Internet Vocabulary | Optional |

# Variations for Younger Children

Children are exposed to the computer at an early age and should become aware of some important social and ethical issues concerning the computer as well as Internet safety. Provide younger children with several opportunities to learn about safety on the Internet, taking into account their various learning styles. Feel free to modify the activities, such as removing a step, to meet the needs of your child. Monitor your child's expression to see if he is showing signs of frustration because the activity is too difficult or signs of boredom because the activity is too easy, then modify the activity to help him succeed on his individual level. You could even make up your own activities. The following ideas may help.

- Concentrate on a few of the Internet safety terms, instead of every term that is discussed throughout the chapter. You may want to expose your child to all of the terms, but focus on one or two terms.

- Allow younger children to use only one website during an activity so it is easier for them to become familiar with the content and navigate the pages. Read the online story to your child while he looks at the pictures.

## Internet Safety

In this chapter, some activities require Internet access. Remind your child to think about Internet safety during these activities. You may want to review the Internet safety tips on pages 10–11.

## Fun Decorations

An inspiring room atmosphere and decorated walls will excite your child and focus his attention on Internet safety. Decorations can generate enthusiasm as well as provide another opportunity to teach your child about safety on the Internet. Be inventive as you plan the room decorations, and remember to have fun! The following ideas might help.

- Print each page of the Internet Safety Slide Show (CD Supplement 2C), glue the words and pictures to construction paper, and then hang them on a wall or door.

- Print and cut out the Internet Safety Cards (CD Supplement 2D), glue them to construction paper, laminate them, and hang them in a creative manner on the wall. You will be ready for Activity 6: Treasure Hunt Game.

- Print, enlarge, and display the Internet Safety Contract (CD Supplement 2E) to be referred to when your child goes over this contract in Activity 8: Contract.

- Dedicate a section of your house to learning about safety on the Internet. Refer to the information located in that area of your home throughout this chapter. Use a banner or letter cutouts to spell out "Safety on the Internet," the topic of this chapter. Hang completed work in this area.

- Write the golden rule on a poster board or a large piece of paper: "Do to others as you would have them do to you." Decorate it with paint or markers. Use this during Activity 3: Golden Rule.

- Change the screensaver or the desktop background of your computer to a picture of one of the safety terms or another graphic that represents Internet safety that your child will be learning in this chapter.

# Vocabulary

Review the following terms with your child so that he or she can have a basic understanding of the vocabulary used in this chapter. You could also have your child write the definitions in the Safety on the Internet Vocabulary worksheet (CD Supplement 2H).

**blog:** A website with a personal journal that is usually updated often. (Short for "Web log.")

**chat room:** A virtual room used to communicate in real time with other people.

**computer virus:** A destructive program that spreads from computer to computer, that may be capable of damaging software and/or erasing your files.

**e-mail:** The exchange of messages using computer networks. (Short for electronic mail.)

**instant messaging:** Messages that are electronically exchanged with another person in real time, using usernames.

**Internet:** A worldwide network connecting millions of computers.

**netiquette:** Appropriate behavior while using the Internet.

**plagiarism:** To use someone else's writing and label it as your own.

**podcast:** Audio and video files that are downloaded from a website to be played on a computer or a mobile device. (Term comes from "iPod" and "broadcasting")

**software:** A program designed for use on computers. For example, Microsoft Word or Mavis Beacon Teaches Typing.

**videoconferencing:** Real-time video and audio communication with two or more people in different locations over the Internet.

**VoIP:** Real-time transmission of voice signals over the Internet. (Voice over Internet Protocol)

# NETS•S Addressed

5. **Digital Citizenship**

   Students understand human, cultural, and societal issues related to technology and practice legal and ethical behavior. Students:

   a. advocate and practice the safe, legal, and responsible use of information and technology

   b. exhibit a positive attitude toward using technology that supports collaboration, learning, and productivity

   c. demonstrate personal responsibility for lifelong learning

   d. exhibit leadership for digital citizenship

# Grades

Think of the best way to determine your child's comprehension of Internet safety concepts for each activity. This is your child's opportunity to demonstrate his individual understanding. Throughout each activity, evaluate your child while he works. When deciding on the type of assessment, consider your child's age and abilities. The following are some suggestions that might help you to assess your child.

- Use the answer keys in the various activities to grade the supplements that your child completed. Base the grades on accuracy or completion.

- Use the Grade Book in Appendix A to record your child's assignments and grades. Keep a running record of your child's progress to determine comprehension and understanding of the content. Record these observations on paper or in the Grade Book.

- Ask your child to write down the definitions to the vocabulary words in this chapter using the Safety on the Internet Vocabulary worksheet (CD Supplement 2H).

- Observe and document the efforts of your children while they are reading online stories, playing games, and using the online dictionaries.

- Have your child memorize the Internet safety song and sing it to you for a grade.

- While your child is playing the online Internet safety game, observe him to ensure that he understands the safety concepts.

- Encourage your child to write down his answers for the questions in Activity 2, based on the story Mr. J. Thaddeus Toad in "Web Mania," and check his answers for correctness or completion.

- Ask your child to write the definition of netiquette along with certain Internet safety rules which could be turned in to be graded.

- Ask your child to turn in his paper with five important concepts learned while playing the Internet safety games in Activity 7 and any other notes taken throughout the chapter.

- Have your child write a paragraph describing the importance of using ethical behavior when online.

# Enrichment

This chapter has provided a foundation in social and ethical concepts surrounding technology. There are also many more safety and netiquette concepts that could be discussed. Brainstorm with your child and find out the topics that he or she is interested in researching. Children could become actively involved by deciding for themselves which enrichment activity to complete. Think of activities to encourage excellent digital citizenship among your children. The following are some suggestions for enrichment activities.

- Suggest that your child think of an interesting technology ethics question based on the concepts learned in this chapter. She could research the answer using the Internet and present her findings to you.

- Have your child teach her friends about the ethical use of technology so that her friends will be aware of Internet safety concepts.

- Have your child search current events to find people who are in trouble for being poor digital citizens.

- Allow your child to interview a neighbor or another adult and ask them questions concerning social and ethical issues related to technology.

- Have your child take SafeKids.com's Online Safety Quiz (www. safekids.com) to determine her Internet safety knowledge.

- Instruct your child to research other Internet safety rules and the importance of these rules.

- Encourage your child to research online to find out about e-mail etiquette.

- Have your child locate a recent news report of an e-mail scheme such as phishing attacks.

- To increase your child's awareness of computer security, ask her to research these security terms: encryption, firewall, clear text, password, hacker, e-commerce, and authentication.

## Closure

Allow a few moments for your child to think about all he has learned concerning safety on the Internet. Your child will take these concepts to be his own as he realizes the social and ethical implications of the proper rules while surfing the Internet. The following are some suggestions for closure activities.

- Ask, "What have you learned concerning safety on the Internet?" and "How is the Internet fun?" Encourage your child to share a few interesting facts or trivia that he has learned about safety on the Internet.

- Encourage your child to share a story or personal experience concerning the concepts learned about the right and wrong way to use a computer.

- Ask about a computer virus: "How can your computer catch one?" and "How can you prevent viruses?"

- Allow your child to play the Internet safety game or listen to the safety song in the future.

Activity **1**

# Internet Safety Song

Easy to
Modify for
Younger Kids

## Goal

Your child will listen to and sing an Internet safety song to learn about being safe online.

## Materials

- SafeKids Online Song Lyrics Slide Show (CD Supplement 2A)
- computer with Internet access
- paper and pencil or word processor (optional)

## Steps

### 1. Prepare

Decide which song will appeal to your child by listening to them in advance.

> **National Crime Prevention Council—McGruff's Internet Safety Song:**
> www.ncpc.org/cms/cms-upload/prevent/files/internet_safety_song_player.swf
>
> **NetSmartz Kids Tunes:** www.netsmartzkids.org/tunes
>
> **SafeKids Online Song:** www.safekids.com/safesong

### 2. Lyrics

Write down or type the lyrics for the song, or, if you decide to use the SafeKids Online Song, open the SafeKids Online Song Lyrics Slide Show (CD Supplement 2A) from the CD using your computer.

### 3. Listen

Play the Internet safety song that you would like your children to listen to. While they are listening to the song, they could read the words that you typed, or if you are using the SafeKids Online Song, they could read the words on the SafeKids Online Song Lyrics Slide Show (CD Supplement 2A).

## 4. Sing

Sing the song along with your child as you play it again while reading the words. Allow your child to listen to it several times so that he really learns the Internet safety concepts.

## 5. Discuss

After listening to the song, have your child share information that he has learned about being safe on the Internet. Encourage your child to share the reasons that it is important for the entire family to be safe when surfing the web.

**Tip**
Have your child memorize the Internet safety song and sing it to you.

Activity **2**

# Online Interactive Stories

## Goal

Your child will watch an online interactive story concerning safety on the Internet.

## Materials

- computer with Internet access
- pencil

## Steps

### 1. Prepare

Listed below are interactive online stories, in Macromedia Flash format, related to ethical behavior while using the computer. Review these websites and choose a developmentally appropriate story for your child to read. This will reinforce the idea of appropriate behavior when using the computer.

**Mr. J. Thaddeus Toad in "Web Mania":**
www2.disney.co.uk/DisneyOnline/Safesurfing/cybernetiquette/netiquette3/

**NetSmartz Kids:** www.netsmartzkids.org/uyn/

**The Peel Children's Safety Village:**
www.peelsafetyvillage.on.ca/kidz/internet.html

**The Three Little Pigs in "Who's Afraid of the Little Sweet Sheep?":**
www2.disney.co.uk/DisneyOnline/Safesurfing/cybernetiquette/netiquette1/

### 2. Show

Show your child the steps to opening and navigating the online story.

## 3. Read

Instruct your child to read an online interactive story at her computer. The story will reinforce social and ethical issues relating to the computer.

## 4. Discuss

Talk with your child about the story and all that she has learned. You may want to write down some questions for your child to answer after she reads the story. Here are some sample questions for the Mr. J. Thaddeus Toad in "Web Mania" online story.

1.  What did Ratty tell Toad?

2.  What is the term for proper behavior on the Internet?

3.  What did Toad promise the weasels?

4.  Why did Toad go to court?

5.  What does it mean when you type in all capital letters on the Internet?

6.  What would you do if you got a chain letter?

7.  What did J. Thaddeus Toad learn?

Activity **3**

# Golden Rule

## Goal

Your child will learn the golden rule and how to be a good digital citizen.

## Materials

- pencil and paper
- crayons, markers, or colored pencils

## Steps

### 1. Prepare

Have your child write this quote on a piece of paper: "Do to others as you would have them do to you." (This is the golden rule.)

### 2. Discuss

Read the golden rule and then use the golden rule to encourage your child to think about right and wrong behavior. Have him give you an example of how he can exemplify the golden rule.

### 3. Story

Tell your child a short story to encourage him to ponder the issue of right and wrong. The following is a sample story that you could read.

*One day a little girl was working on the computer in the computer lab. The teacher finished explaining the instructions for playing an online Internet game, but the girl still did not understand the way to open the game. You are sitting next to her, and you are already playing the game. What should you do?*

## 4. Digital Citizen

Talk about the meaning of integrity and why it is important to be responsible for your actions all the time, even when using technology. Explain that if people think something they are going to do is wrong, it is better to just not do it. Discuss consequences of things that could happen when people are not good digital citizens and potentially break the law.

## 5. Draw

Have your child draw a picture on his paper showing something that he can do to show the golden rule. Examples:

- share toys with a friend
- serve others before yourself when passing out snacks
- help someone who dropped their books
- do not send viruses to other people
- be kind to others when typing online

He could use crayons, markers, or colored pencils to color his picture.

**Tips**

Allow your child to watch video clips, read stories, and play games while learning about many character traits at Auto-B-Good (www.autobgood.com), a Rising Star Education site. Auto-B-Good is an Emmy Award–winning character education program and has a character development curriculum for schools.

Have your child watch character education videos that reinforce the idea of ethical behavior using one of the hundreds of videos available from Nest Learning (www.nestlearning.com/character-education_c1542.aspx).

Activity 4

# Internet Safety Terms

## Goal

Your child will look up the definition of 11 Internet safety terms and record them on a worksheet.

## Materials

- Internet Safety Terms Worksheet (CD Supplement 2B)
- computer with Internet access
- pencil

## Steps

### 1. Prepare

Here are several online dictionaries that could be used to locate the definition of a specific Internet safety term. Become familiar with the websites ahead of time so that you can decide which sites will be best for your child.

**Dictionary.com:** www.dictionary.com

**Merriam-Webster:** www.m-w.com/home.htm

**Your Dictionary:** www.yourdictionary.com

### 2. Teach

Show your child how to navigate the website and ways to look up a term using an online dictionary. You may want to locate one of the terms together with your child by typing the term in the search box.

### 3. Worksheet

Explain how your child can find the definitions using the online dictionaries and record them on Internet Safety Terms worksheet (CD Supplement 2B). Have your child write the meanings of the terms using her own words.

## 4. *Check*

When your child has completed the worksheet, discuss each term to ensure that your child has written down the correct answer according to the vocabulary definitions listed at the beginning of this chapter. While reviewing the definitions, you could also discuss things that your child should do in the Do ☺ column and things she should not do in the Don't ☹ column in the chart on the following page.

**Tips**
Use a printed dictionary to look up the terms instead of using an online dictionary. Show your child the printed dictionary and discuss the similarities to and differences from an online dictionary.

| Term | Do ☺ | Don't ☹ |
| --- | --- | --- |
| Software | Do buy your own software. | Do not make copies of software and pass them out to your friends. |
| Computer Virus | Do delete viruses from your computer. | Do not send viruses to other people. |
| Plagiarism | Do read information and then put it in your own words. | Do not copy straight from the Internet. |
| E-mail | Do be polite when sending e-mail. | Do not send chain mail. |
| Internet | Do go to safe places on the Internet approved by your parents. | Do not surf to bad websites. |
| Podcast | Do download and listen to music and podcasts from safe sites. | Do not download anything that your parents don't approve. |
| Instant Messaging | Do send IMs when given permission to communicate online. | Do not send IMs when you are having a conversation with another person. |
| Chat Room | Do talk in chat rooms about your opinions while using a username. | Do not give away personal information about yourself. |
| Blog | Do visit a blog when it is part of a learning assignment. | Do not read or post comments on blogs without your parents' permission. |
| Videoconferencing | Do look at the camera and stay focused on the videoconference. | Do not videoconference with strangers. |
| VoIP | Do talk with your friends and family using good phone call manners. | Do not interrupt or do distracting things during a conference call. |
| Netiquette | Do remember the golden rule when communicating online. | Do not use bad behavior when communicating online. |

Activity **5**

Easy to
Modify for
Younger Kids

# Internet Safety Slide Show

## Goal

Your child will watch a slide show and learn more about the Internet safety terms.

## Materials

- Internet Safety Slide Show (CD Supplement 2C)
- computer

## Steps

### 1. Prepare

Open the Internet Safety Slide Show (CD Supplement 2C).
Click Slide Show > View Slide Show when you are ready to begin.

### 2. Assess

As you advance each slide, have your child identify any of the terms that he knows while watching the slide show, which shows a picture and the name of the term. This is a great way to assess the information your child has about the Internet safety terms.

### 3. Details

Play the slide show again and discuss the terms and provide more insightful knowledge. Details as well as some informative websites are provided in the following chart. The specific issues focused on during this activity should be chosen carefully to meet the needs of your child at his current level of understanding and technology expertise. Your child could advance the slides during the multimedia presentation.

## Software

The following list describes five types of software.

1. **Commercial Products.** Software bought from stores.

2. **Shareware.** Copyrighted, but users are allowed to try it before buying it (shareware.com).

3. **Freeware.** Copyrighted, distributed freely in the hope that someone will find it useful (freeware.com).

4. **Public Domain.** Not copyrighted, free because people already own it in some capacity anyway.

5. **Open Source.** Free and open source software (FOSS). Free software that allows everyone to modify the program code to better suit their needs.

## Computer Virus

These questions and answers should help your child understand a computer virus.

**Question:** How can your computer catch a virus?

**Answer:** You can receive a virus through e-mail, software, compact discs, or USB drives, or by downloading files from the Internet.

**Question:** How can you protect your computer from viruses?

**Answer:** You should scan your computer often with virus protection software, such as Norton Antivirus or MacAfee.

**Question:** Why do people write computer viruses?

**Answer:** It may be difficult to answer this question. Try answering this question with another question: Why do people vandalize property, rob banks, or steal things? Programmers may write viruses to find out the number of computers their virus can destroy.

## Plagiarism

These websites have a lot of information on plagiarism.

**Why Students Plagiarize:** www.library.ualberta.ca/guides/plagiarism/

**How Not to Plagiarize:**
www.writing.utoronto.ca/advice/using-sources/how-not-to-plagiarize

## E-mail

The ISTE publication *Safe Practices for Life Online* by Doug Fodeman and Marje Monroe (www.iste.org/LIFEON/) offers a wealth of information about appropriate and ethical e-mail practices.

## Internet

The Learn the Net website (http://learnthenet.com) could be used to teach your child more about the Internet. An online, animated self-tutorial describes the workings of the Internet (www.learnthenet.com/english/section/www.html).

The HowStuffWorks website describes how the Internet works in more detail (www.howstuffworks.com/category.htm?cat=Intrnt).

## Podcasts

This Creative Commons website offers a Podcasting Legal Guide (http://wiki.creativecommons.org/Podcasting_Legal_Guide). If using headphones, remind children to keep the volume down to protect their hearing.

## Instant Messaging

SafeKids.com (http://safekids.com) has lots of information on Internet safety as well as the SafeKids Song.

Links to several sites with topics such as CyberSmart Manners and CyberSmart Safety can be found at www.cybersmartcurriculum.org/safetysecurity/homeconnection/.

## Chat Rooms, Blogs, Videoconferencing, and VoIP

Be sure to teach your child that these communications methods could be very dangerous for children if they are not familiar with Internet safety techniques.

General communications information for kids can be found in the "Kid's Guide to Etiquette on the Net" (www.kidsdomain.com/brain/computer/surfing/netiquette_kids.html) and the Boston Public Library's Netiquette for Kids page (www.bpl.org/kids/netiquette.htm).

## 4. Write

Your child should have a good understanding of Internet safety and the correct way to behave when using technology. Instruct your child to write down five important ethical actions to remember when using computers.

**Tip**
The Family Contract for Online Safety: Kids' Pledge is discussed in more detail in Activity 9: Contract.

Activity **6**

# Treasure Hunt Game

## Goal

Your child will play a game in which an Internet safety term is matched to the card with the correct definition.

## Materials

- Internet Safety Cards (CD Supplement 2D)
- scissors
- tape
- construction paper (optional)

## Steps

### 1. Prepare

Print and cut out the Internet Safety Cards (CD Supplement 2D). Glue them to construction paper for added durability.

### 2. Review

Before you begin, you may want to review the terms and definitions with your child.

### 3. Position Cards

Tape all of the picture cards with the terms at different locations around your house. Place all of the definition cards in a stack next to your child.

### 4. Play

Your child will go on a fun treasure hunt to tape the cards next to the correct term. Your child will choose one card at a time, read the definition, locate the correct term, and then tape the definition next to it.

For example, if your child reads the definition "A virtual room used to communicate in real time with other people," then she should locate the chat room card and tape the definition next to that card.

## 5. *Check*

Use the definitions given in the vocabulary section at the beginning of this chapter to check and make sure your child has placed all of the cards next to the correct terms.

**Tips**
For added fun, attach a small treasure or treat to some of the picture cards for your child to enjoy when she locates the correct card. You may want to leave these cards hanging up so your child can view them for a few days.

Activity **7**

# Internet Safety Games

Easy to
Modify for
Younger Kids

## Goal

Your child will play an online Internet safety game.

## Materials

- computer with Internet access
- paper and pencil

## Steps

### 1. Prepare

Listed below are several Internet safety games that your child could play to learn more about being safe online. Review these websites and choose a developmentally appropriate game for your child to play. This will reinforce the idea of appropriate behavior when using the computer.

**KidsCom:** www.kidscom.com/games/isg/isg.html

**Looney Tunes Teach the Internet:**
http://looneytunes2.warnerbros.com/ltti/homepage.html

**McGruff Internet Safety:** www.mcgruff.org/Games/is.php

**NetSmartz Kids:** www.netsmartzkids.org/games/

**Safety Land:** www.att.com/Common/images/safety/game.html

**Surf Swell Island Adventures in Internet Safety:**
http://home.disney.com.au/activities/surfswellisland/

### 2. Show

Show your child the steps to opening and navigating the game and activities. The detail of instruction will depend on the grade level of your child.

### 3. *Play*

Instruct your child to play the game at his computer. The games reinforce social and ethical issues relating to the computer.

### 4. *Discuss*

Talk with your child about the game and all that he has learned. Have him note five important concepts learned about Internet safety and record them on paper or type them into a word processing document.

Activity 8

# Contract

Easy to
Modify for
Younger Kids

## Goal

Your child will read and sign an Internet safety contract.

## Materials

- Internet Safety Contract (CD Supplement 2E)
- pencil

## Steps

### 1. Prepare

Print out the Internet Safety Contract (CD Supplement 2E) from the CD.

### 2. Read

Read and discuss the contract with your child.

1. I will not give out personal information such as my address, telephone number, parents' work address/telephone number, or the name and location of my school without my parents' permission.

2. I will tell my parents right away if I come across any information that makes me feel uncomfortable.

3. I will never agree to get together with someone I meet online without first checking with my parents. If my parents agree to the meeting, I will be sure that it is in a public place and bring my mother or father along.

4. I will never send a person my picture or anything else without first checking with my parents.

5. I will not respond to any messages that are mean or in any way make me feel uncomfortable. It is not my fault if I get a message like that. If I do I will tell my parents right away so that they can contact the service provider.

6. I will talk with my parents so that we can set up rules for going online. We will decide upon the time of day that I can be online, the length of time I can be online, and appropriate areas for me to visit. I will not access other areas or break these rules without their permission.

7. I will not give out my Internet password to anyone (even my best friends) other than my parents.

8. I will check with my parents before downloading or installing software or doing anything that could possibly hurt our computer or jeopardize my family's privacy.

9. I will be a good online citizen and not do anything that hurts other people or is against the law.

10. I will help my parents understand how to have fun and learn things online and teach them things about the Internet, computers, and other technology.

*(Source: Kids' Rules for Online Safety, © 2005 Larry Magrid, SafeKids.com)*

## 3. Sign

Sign the contract and talk to your child about what it means to sign an important document.

> **Tip**
> For the Parents' Pledge and for more information about the Family Contract for Online Safety, visit SafeKids.com (www.safekids.com).

Activity 9

# Netiquette

## Goal

Your child will make a netiquette poster.

## Materials

- posterboard and markers or paint

## Steps

### 1. Define

Discuss the term "netiquette" with your child. Netiquette is simply appropriate behavior while using the Internet.

### 2. Share

Have your child share ways he can use appropriate behavior when using the Internet.

### 3. Write

Allow your child to write the term and definition on a large piece of posterboard using markers or paint.

### 4. Illustrate

Give your child some time to be creative and let him illustrate the poster with decorations and pictures.

**Tips**
On the poster, your child could write a list of things he can do to be safe when online. He could write some consequences that could happen if he does not use appropriate behavior when using the Internet.

Activity **10**

# *Quiz*

## Goal

Your child will take a quiz on the Internet safety terms.

## Materials

- Internet Safety Quiz (CD Supplement 2F)
- Internet Safety Quiz Answers (CD Supplement 2G)
- computer or pencil

## Steps

### 1. *Prepare*

Open and print the Internet Safety Quiz (CD Supplement 2F). For something different, allow your child to take the quiz on your computer by opening the quiz there. She could then type the letters into the boxes to show her answers.

### 2. *Quiz*

Explain the instructions at the top of the assessment. Give your child enough time to take the quiz. Go over any questions.

### 3. *Check*

Use the Internet Safety Quiz Answers (CD Supplement 2G) to grade your child's work. Go over any missed questions with your child.

## Chapter 3

# Keyboarding

## Objective

Children will demonstrate the correct keyboarding and finger positions and type with increasing accuracy by participating in many different keyboarding activities.

## Purpose

Provide your child with a rationale for learning to type correctly. Explain that it is important to know the correct keyboarding position to be able to type efficiently and without injury (see the section on ergonomics in the Introduction). If the importance of typing correctly is conveyed to children in a way that inspires them, they will be motivated to learn the proper techniques. Children need to fully understand the importance of learning to type to gain a sense of urgency to learn. This urgent feeling will drive them to practice until mastery is complete. Give children the coaching and the time to practice they need to successfully learn to type.

## Activities Overview

This chapter will expand your child's typing abilities and promote the correct keyboarding position through a variety of activities. Carefully consider which activities will benefit your child depending on his or her age, abilities, and learning styles. Some children may be able to complete all of the activities, while others would benefit from focusing more time on a few key activities.

Your children should work at their own pace and really understand the concepts. You may want to repeat an activity or allow your child more time on a certain activity, such as Activity 6, when your child practices typing. To get started, you may decide to plan a fun activity to inspire your child and focus your child's attention on keyboarding. A lively event will prompt children to focus on the keyboarding, and they will be more interested and ready to learn.

The following chart lists and categorizes each activity to help you to plan the lessons. For example, if you feel that your child would learn best with a game at a particular time, then choose an activity in the game column.

| Activities | Worksheet | Modifiable* | Internet Access | Game | Learning Cards | Slide Show | Arts and Crafts | Answer Key |
|---|---|---|---|---|---|---|---|---|
| 1. Keyboarding Position | ✔ | ✔ | | | | | | ✔ |
| 2. Learn the Keys | | | | | ✔ | | | |
| 3. Keyboard Chart | ✔ | ✔ | | | | | ✔ | ✔ |
| 4. Keyboard Styles | | ✔ | ✔ | | | | | |
| 5. WPM | ✔ | | | | | | | |
| 6. Practice Typing | | | ✔ | | | | | |
| 7. Keyboard Chart Game | ✔ | | | ✔ | | | | ✔ |
| 8. Typing Game | | ✔ | | ✔ | | | | |
| 9. Quiz | ✔ | ✔ | | | | | | ✔ |
| 10. Test | ✔ | | | | | | | ✔ |

* Easily modifiable for younger children

## CD Supplements

The following chart lists all of the CD supplements for this chapter and provides the CD filename, supplement title, and activity number. To make locating and using these supplements faster and easier, it is recommended that you copy all files to your hard drive before beginning the lessons.

| CD Filename | Title | Activity |
|---|---|---|
| 3A | Correct Keyboarding Position | 1 |
| 3B | Correct Keyboarding Position Answers | 1 |
| 3C | Keyboarding Slide Show | 2 |
| 3D | Keyboard Chart Worksheet | 3, 7 |
| 3E | Keyboard Chart Answers | 3, 7 |
| 3F | WPM Recording Sheet | 5 |
| 3G | Keyboarding Quiz I | 9 |
| 3H | Keyboarding Quiz II | 9 |
| 3I | Keyboarding Quiz I Answers | 9 |
| 3J | Keyboarding Quiz II Answers | 9 |
| 3K | Keyboard Test | 10 |
| 3L | Keyboard Test Answers | 10 |
| 3M | Keyboarding Vocabulary | Optional |

## Variations for Younger Children

Provide younger children with several opportunities to learn keyboarding skills, taking into account their various learning styles. For younger children, learning the correct keyboarding technique may be more important than increasing the typing speed. Think about the amount of actual keyboarding practice that is appropriate for your child to maximize your child's potential and minimize frustration. Feel free to modify the activities, such as removing a step, to meet the needs of your child. Monitor your child's expression to see if he is showing signs of frustration because the activity is too difficult or signs of boredom because the activity is too easy then modify the activity to help him succeed on his individual level. You could even make up your own activities. The following ideas may help.

- Carefully choose a typing application suitable for younger children or a website from the keyboarding websites provided in this chapter.

- Choose one website for younger children to use when typing online. Several of the sites include games and simple typing activities.

- Have children type the alphabet using a simple word processor.

- Have children type only the alphabetical letters that they are able to easily recognize.

- Expose children who are still learning to read to the correct keyboarding position. It may be developmentally inappropriate for some younger children to type for 20 minutes using a typing program.

- Have children type in all caps or in all lowercase instead of capitalizing words, because it may be too difficult or take too long for them to simultaneously press the shift key and another key.

- Have younger children type on a word processor using the Caps Lock both on and off to see the function of this key.

- Have children use the keyboard to type their first name in a simple word processor. This will expose them to the appropriate use of the keyboard. This may be the first time some children have used a keyboard; typing their name to be seen on the screen will be very exciting!

- Verbally call out one or two letters and have children practice typing those letters over and over again. Do this exercise using different patterns of these letters.

- Have younger children use the keyboard to type a short sentence in a simple word processor.

- Complete the quiz and test together with the younger child.

- Instruct children to write down the home row keys on a piece of paper and turn it in for a grade.

## Internet Safety

In this chapter, some activities require Internet access. Remind your child to think about Internet safety during these activities. You may want to review the Internet safety tips on pages 10–11.

## Fun Decorations

An inspiring room atmosphere and decorated walls will excite your children and focus their attention on keyboarding. Decorations can generate enthusiasm as well as provide another opportunity to teach keyboarding skills. Be creative in assembling decorations to motivate your children to learn about keyboarding. The following are some ideas that might help you with decorations.

- Print each page of the Keyboarding Slide Show (CD Supplement 3C), glue the words and pictures to construction paper, and then hang them on a wall or door.

- Print out and enlarge a graphic of the correct keyboarding position from the Correct Keyboarding Position Worksheet (CD Supplement 3A). Display it next to the computer.

- Print in color the Keyboard Chart Answers (CD Supplement 3E) and display it at your computer or at a strategic location around the room that can be easily seen by your child when typing. Try to place this color-coded keyboard next to the monitor so your child can look at it without looking down when typing.

- Create a large poster of the keyboard from the Keyboard Chart Answers (CD Supplement 3E). Enlarge this to approximately four feet long using an enlarging machine and display it on a wall. Enlarging machines can be found at art or office supply stores.

- Enlarge the keyboard from the Keyboard Chart (CD Supplement 3D) to make an interactive keyboard. This enlarged interactive keyboard can be used in a variety of ways. If you wish to emphasize only a few keys at a time, add those colored keys to the display. This allows your child to clearly see the keys being taught. This display could also be used to illustrate the home row keys by adding just those colored keys to the background keyboard. As an exercise, pass out the keys and ask your child to place the correct keys on the keyboard.

- Follow these steps to create a fun keyboard to use in a variety of ways throughout the chapter. This decoration can be used in Activity 7: Keyboard Chart Game.

  1. Enlarge the keyboard on an enlarging machine two times and create two copies exactly the same size, approximately four feet long.

  2. Laminate and display one of the keyboards. To make the keyboard stronger, attach it to a poster board before or after laminating.

  3. Color the keys of the second keyboard to correspond with the colors on the Keyboard Chart Answers (CD Supplement 3E). Construction paper, paint, markers, crayons, or colored pencils could be used to color the keys.

  4. Laminate and cut out the colored keys from the second keyboard.

  5. Attach Velcro squares or small magnets to the back of the cut-out keys and to the corresponding spot on the keys on the first keyboard.

  6. Attach the colored keys to the large keyboard on display and remove them to clearly demonstrate the correct fingering positions.

- Dedicate a section of your house to learning about keyboarding. Refer to the information located in that area of your home throughout this chapter. Use a banner or letter cutouts to spell out "Keyboarding," the topic of this chapter. Hang your child's completed work in this area.

- Change the screensaver or the desktop background of your computer to a picture of a keyboard.

## Vocabulary

Review the following terms with your child so that he or she can have a basic understanding of the vocabulary used in this chapter. You could also have your child write the definitions in the Keyboarding Vocabulary worksheet (CD Supplement 3M).

> **home row keys:** The keys on the keyboard where your fingers rest when you are not typing. A S D F J K L ; .
>
> **keyboarding:** To input text into a computer using a keyboard.

# NETS•S Addressed

6. **Technology Operations and Concepts**

   Students demonstrate a sound understanding of technology concepts, systems, and operations. Students:

   a. understand and use technology systems

   b. select and use applications effectively and productively

   c. troubleshoot systems and applications

   d. transfer current knowledge to the learning of new technologies

# Grades

Think of the best way to determine your child's comprehension of the keyboarding for each activity. This is your child's opportunity to demonstrate her individual understanding of keyboarding. Throughout each activity, evaluate your child while she works. When deciding on the type of assessment, consider her age and abilities. The following are some suggestions that might help you to assess your child.

- Use the answer keys in the various activities to grade the supplements that your child completed. Base the grades on accuracy or completion. The answer keys can be found on the CD.

- You may want to use the Grade Book located in Appendix A at the back of this book to record your child's assignments and grades.

- Keep a running record of your child's progress to determine comprehension and understanding of the content. Record these observations on paper or in the Grade Book (Appendix A).

- Ask your child to write down the definitions to the vocabulary words in this chapter using the Keyboarding Vocabulary worksheet (CD Supplement 3M), which could be graded.

- Assess your child's typing improvement by giving a keyboarding posttest, which could be compared with a pretest.

- If the typing application used in the chapter has an evaluation component, implement this test as a keyboarding assessment.

- Assign daily keyboarding practice. Make a chart for your child to mark after practicing each day.

- Have your child write the function of certain keys on paper or type them into a word processor for future reference.

# Enrichment

The excitement will probably show on your child's face as he learns to type. A spark may have been ignited. Offer activities that will enhance your children's current typing skills and challenge them. Children could become actively involved by deciding for themselves which enrichment activity to complete, causing them to really take ownership of the information. Be creative in planning and implementing something that your child will never forget. The following are some suggestions for enrichment activities.

- Encourage your child to be creative and design his own keyboard, and then type a short paragraph explaining the keyboard.

- Have your child compose a song or verse that helps him memorize the home row position or the correct finger assignment for keys.

- Have your child create a chart showing individual keyboarding improvement throughout the chapter. Your child could also record the amount of time practiced each day.

- Videotape your child while typing. Then watch the video together and discuss the correct keyboarding position.

- Set typing goals with your child. Require your child to spend a set amount of time every day typing.

- Give your child a typing assignment such as typing a poem, a letter, spelling words, or a recipe to improve his keyboarding skills.

- Play typing games to motivate your child and increase his typing abilities.

- Talk with a family member, neighbor, or friend who types regularly and talk about the importance of typing using the correct position. Ask them to share their personal experiences with typing.

- Have your child research and explain the differences between Apple and PC keyboards.

# Closure

Your children will find satisfaction in knowing they have typed to the best of their ability. Be honest and tell them how they did while typing. Well-deserved praise will encourage and bolster their confidence when typing. The closing of each chapter is an important part of the learning process because children are given a few minutes to reflect on all they have learned and make the information their own. Choose one or more of the following ideas to complete this chapter.

- Share your child's typing speed increase using the WPM Recording Sheet (CD Supplement 3F).

- Have a "keyboarding celebration" when you give your child a certificate for keyboarding practice. Invite a special relative or friend to congratulate your child on her typing skills.

- Take pictures of your child when typing to be printed and displayed.

- Require your child to be accountable for knowing the keys on the keyboard in a few weeks.

- Ask, "What have you learned about keyboarding?" Encourage your child to share a few interesting facts or trivia that she has learned about keyboarding.

Throughout the year, refer to the typing skills your child learned in this keyboarding chapter. Have your children practice typing when they have extra time to increase accuracy and speed.

Activity **1**

# Keyboarding Position

Easy to
Modify for
Younger Kids

## Goal

Your child will demonstrate the correct keyboarding position and then complete a worksheet.

## Materials

- Correct Keyboarding Position (CD Supplement 3A)
- Correct Keyboarding Position Answers (CD Supplement 3B)
- computer
- chair

## Steps

### 1. Keyboarding Position

Explain to your child the proper way to sit when typing at the computer. Or, show your child the correct keyboarding position by sitting at the computer yourself.

- Eyes on monitor
- Wrists flat
- Fingers curved
- Feet flat on floor
- Back straight
- Fingers on home row position

### 2. Demonstrate

Allow your child to demonstrate the proper way to sit when typing. If your child is not sitting correctly, reinforce the correct position by referring to the picture on the worksheet of the typist sitting correctly. Encourage correct posture at the computer to eliminate pain and strain, as well as to establish lifelong healthy habits.

## 3. Worksheet

Have your child complete the Correct Keyboarding Position worksheet (CD Supplement 3A) by filling in the blanks.

## 4. Check

Use the Correct Keyboarding Position Answers (CD Supplement 3B) to check your child's work. Your child could also use the answer key to self-check his work.

**Tips**

Hang the worksheet close to your computer so that your child can refer to the correct keyboarding position when needed. Ask, "Why is it important to sit correctly?" Have your child respond. Sample answer: It is important to sit correctly so that your arms, wrists, and back are not injured.

Activity **2**

# *Learn the Keys*

## Goal

Your child will learn the home row keys and other important keys during a slide show presentation.

## Materials

- Keyboarding Slide Show (CD Supplement 3C)
- keyboard

## Steps

### 1. Prepare

Open the Keyboarding Slide Show (CD Supplement 3C).
Click Slide Show > View Slide Show when you are ready to begin.

### 2. Home Row

Instruct your child on the home row position. Click the mouse to view each home row key on the slide show. Have your child say the letters as they appear. If necessary, repeat the home row keys and have your child place her fingers and thumbs correctly on the keyboard. Explain that certain fingers rest on certain keys when typing (see the list below). Tell your child that the thumbs are always on the spacebar.

- Pinkies on **A** and **;**
- Ring fingers on **S** and **L**
- Middle fingers on **D** and **K**
- Index fingers on **F** and **J**
- Thumbs on **Spacebar**

## 3. Frequently Used Keys

During the slide show discuss the function of each key listed in the chart below. Allow your child to locate the key on her individual keyboard. Explain that certain keys perform specific functions on the keyboard.

| Key | Function |
|---|---|
| Backspace | Deletes a character to the left of the cursor |
| Caps Lock | Capitalizes all letters |
| Delete | Deletes a character to the right of the cursor |
| Enter | 1. Completes a command<br>2. Moves cursor down to the next line |
| Shift | 1. Capitalizes letters<br>2. Inserts symbols<br>Press and hold the Shift key, then press another key to capitalize a letter or to insert a symbol |
| Tab | Indents |

**Tips**

Have your child write down the information on the slides for future reference. Discuss other keys on the keyboard such as Num Lock, function keys, arrows, Ctrl, Alt, Page Up, Page Down, Home, End, Insert, Print Screen, Scroll Lock, and Pause Break. If your child is using an Apple keyboard, discuss the Command, Option, and Delete keys. Ask your child to write the home row keys on paper before they are revealed on the slide show. This will allow your child to self-check her knowledge of the home row keys.

Have your child describe the function of the keys in his own words. Remind your child of the reason for the raised bumps on certain keys. The raised bumps help a typist find the correct home row position by feeling for these bumps without looking down at the keyboard.

Activity **3**

# Keyboard Chart

Easy to
Modify for
Younger Kids

## Goal

Your child will complete and then discuss the Keyboard Chart worksheet.

## Materials

- Keyboard Chart Worksheet (CD Supplement 3D)
- Keyboard Chart Answers (CD Supplement 3E)
- crayons, colored pencils, or markers

## Steps

### 1. Chart

Instruct your child to color the keys on the Keyboard Chart Worksheet (CD Supplement 3D) the correct color using crayons, colored pencils, or markers and answer the question at the bottom of the page.

### 2. Check

Check your child's work using the Keyboard Chart Answers (CD Supplement 3E) to ensure that your child has colored everything correctly. Go over the answer to the question "What are the home row keys?" located at the bottom of the worksheet. Answer: A S D F J K L ;

### 3. Visualize

Have your child place his fingers on the keyboard chart to visually understand which fingers press which keys on the keyboard. Say the name of a specific key out loud and have your child place the correct finger on the corresponding key on the keyboard chart. This activity allows your child to see that certain fingers go with certain keys on the keyboard.

## 4. Patterns

Ask, "What are the color patterns on your keyboard chart?" Your child may look on his own worksheet and give a few different responses. Sample answers may include: 6, 3, 3, 6, 6, 3, 3, 6; or diagonal steps slanted to the right; or various other patterns found on the keyboard.

**Tips**

While your child is looking at the Keyboarding Chart Answers (CD Supplement 3E), encourage him to be creative in figuring out some tricks to remember the fingers and their corresponding keys. For example, the left middle finger is assigned to the E, D, and C keys, and DEC is the abbreviation for the month of December. Also, many of the keys for the left index finger sound alike, such as T, G, B, and V. Your child will have fun thinking of tips to remember the finger positions.

Activity 4

# Keyboard Styles

Easy to
Modify for
Younger Kids

## Goal

Your child will view different styles of keyboards.

## Materials

- keyboard
- computer with Internet access

## Steps

### 1. Sound

Have your child close her eyes as you type on the keyboard. Then ask your child to share what she hears while her eyes are closed. Or, go to a clip art gallery for this sound effect or do an online search for "typing sound," and play the sound for your child to hear. Tell her that there are many keyboards with different styles and sounds.

### 2. View

Go online and do a quick search for various computer keyboard types and allow your child to view the different keyboard styles. Explain that there are many different types of computer keyboards available including ergonomic, portable, and bendable. Each keyboard has a different look and feel to it. You may want to allow your child to type on several different types of keyboards at home or at a store that sells keyboards. Ask you child which keyboard she likes the best.

### 3. Discuss

Talk to your child about the advantages and disadvantages of the various keyboard designs. Explain that sometimes people need small, portable keyboards so they can carry them and use the keyboard away from home. Others may want a backlight on the keyboard so they can easily view the keys as they work. Some people need a full-sized keyboard with a numeric pad to quickly type numbers. Some may like a keyboard with an integrated mouse.

Activity **5**

# WPM

## Goal

Your child will take a WPM (words per minute) test and record his typing speed.

## Materials

- WPM Recording Sheet (CD Supplement 3F)
- computer with Internet access
- pencil

## Steps

### 1. Prepare

Listed below are several websites that could be used to take a WPM test. Become familiar with the websites ahead of time so that you can decide which sites will best meet the abilities of your child.

**Free Typing Game Tests:** www.freetypinggame.net/free-typing-test.asp

**Learn 2 Type Test:** www.learn2type.com/TypingTest

**Typing Master Test:** www.typingtest.com

### 2. Test

Show your child how to take the WPM typing test using a website. If you have a typing program installed on your computer, you may want to use a WPM test included with that software.

## 3. Record

Record your child's score on the WPM Recording Sheet (CD Supplement 3F). Continue to use this same WPM test to show your child's typing progress over the next few weeks.

**Tips**
You may want to place a manila folder or a large piece of paper on top of your child's hands so he cannot see the keyboard while typing. It would be ideal to purchase a keyboard cover made for your particular style of keyboard. The plastic, flexible keyboard cover fits on top of the keys so your child can easily type, but is unable to see the characters on the keys. Make a line chart or bar graph displaying your child's typing progress.

Activity **6**

# Practice Typing

## Goal

Your child will practice typing independently using a website or software.

## Materials

- A computer with Internet access or a typing program such as Type to Learn or Mavis Beacon Teaches Typing.

## Steps

### 1. Prepare

Listed below are several websites that could be used to practice typing. Choose the one that will be the best for your child's age and current keyboarding skills. Become familiar with the websites or software of your choice ahead of time so that you will know how to use the application.

**Dance Mat Typing:** www.bbc.co.uk/schools/typing/

**Free Typing Game:** www.freetypinggame.net/play.asp

**Julia's Rainbow Corner:** www.juliasrainbowcorner.com/html/typing.html

**Kids Domain Computer Connections:**
www.kidsdomain.com/brain/computer/type.html

**Typing Master:** www.typingmaster.com

**Typing Master Typing Games:**
www.typingtest.com/games/default.asp?m=1

### 2. Type

Show your child how to type independently using the typing application or website of your choice. Reinforce the idea that speed is not currently important; your child should concentrate on developing and practicing fundamental typing skills. Dim the lights as your child types to minimize the glare on the monitor.

### 3. Observe

Carefully observe your child during keyboarding practice to ensure that correct skills are demonstrated, especially correct fingering. An incorrect fingering position will be difficult to correct in the future. While your child is keyboarding, remind her of the correct keyboarding position. You may need to model the correct position and encourage your child to sit correctly. Allow your child to refer to a keyboard poster hanging close to the monitor, if needed.

### 4. Break

After a period of typing, give your child a break with a few stretching exercises. This will emphasize the importance of taking breaks while keyboarding.

**Tips**
It may be helpful to keep a copy of the Keyboard Chart Answers (CD Supplement 3E) next to the computer monitor for your child to refer to while typing. Allow your child to play a typing game for fun after practicing typing for a period of time. If your child keeps looking at her fingers, remember to use a manila folder, a large piece of paper, or a keyboard cover.

Activity **7**

# Keyboard Chart Game

## Goal

Your child will place keys in the correct place to put together a keyboard.

## Materials

- Keyboard Chart (CD Supplement 3D)
- Keyboard Chart Answers (CD Supplement 3E)
- scissors, tape

## Steps

### 1. Prepare

You or your child will cut out the colored keys from the Keyboard Chart Answers (CD Supplement 3E).

### 2. Assess

Give your child the colored keys one at a time and ask him to place the keys in the correct place on the Keyboard Chart (CD Supplement 3D). You may want to have your child label the keyboard by taping the colored keys in place. Have your child share which fingers go with which keys.

### 3. Check

Check each key to see if your child put the card in the correct place. If your child needs extra practice, do the activity again.

**Tips**

Encourage your child memorize the placement of the keys on the keyboard. Do this activity using the enlarged keyboard as described in the Fun Decorations section. Ask your child to tell you the function of some special keys, such as Tab, Shift, and Caps Lock. Have your child try to put the keys in the correct place on a blank piece of paper.

Easy to
Modify for
Younger Kids

Activity **8**

# Typing Game

## Goal

Your child will play a game in which she types the letters that you say.

## Materials

- A computer with a word processor

## Steps

### 1. Review

Before you begin, review the correct keyboarding position with your child.

### 2. Type

Have your child close her eyes and type the letters that you say, such as "ASDF JKL;." Repeat the letters in different orders and speeds over and over again to help her memorize the finger position for the key. Start with one or two letters, and then continue with more letters when your child is ready.

### 3. Check

When you are finished, have your child open her eyes and read the letters on her screen as you repeat them to check and see if she typed the correct letters.

**Tips**
Play this game by calling out words, instead of letters. When your child is ready for even more advanced games, include numbers, symbols, capital letters, and even sentences, such as "I love _____" (your child can type something she loves).

Activity **9**

# Quiz

Easy to
Modify for
Younger Kids

## Goal

Your child will take a keyboarding quiz.

## Materials

- Keyboarding Quiz I or II (CD Supplement 3G or 3H)
- Keyboarding Quiz I or II Answers (CD Supplement 3I or 3J)
- computer or pencil

## Steps

### 1. Prepare

Decide which Keyboarding Quiz (I or II) will best meet the needs of your child. Print out the appropriate quiz (CD Supplement 3G or 3H).

### 2. Quiz

Explain the instructions at the top of the assessment. Give your child enough time to take the quiz to determine all that he has learned about keyboarding during this chapter. Go over any questions.

### 3. Check

Use the Keyboarding Quiz I or II Answers (CD Supplement 3I or 3J) to grade your child's work. Go over any missed questions with your child.

Activity **10**

# *Test*

## Goal

Your child will write in the keys on a blank keyboard.

## Materials

- Keyboard Test (CD Supplement 3K)
- Keyboard Test Answers (CD Supplement 3L)
- pencil

## Steps

### 1. Prepare

Print out the Keyboard Test (CD Supplement 3K).

### 2. Test

Explain the instructions at the top of the test. Go over any questions. Have your child take the test, giving her enough time to complete it.

### 3. Check

Use the Keyboard Test Answers (CD Supplements 3L) to grade your child's work. Go over any missed keys with your child.

## Chapter 4

# The World Wide Web

## Objective

Children will learn about basic navigation on the World Wide Web, Internet infrastructure, URLs (Uniform Resource Locators), web browsers, IP (Internet Protocol) addresses, download speeds, switches, and hubs.

## Purpose

At the completion of this chapter, your child should have a sound understanding of how the Internet works and how to navigate the World Wide Web. Provide personal meaning about the World Wide Web to your children by encouraging them to take ownership of the information so that they will be committed to learning. For example, the online learning tutorials could be their first exposure to an online class. Some children take similar online classes through a home school environment. Many adults earn a college degree by taking online courses. Furthermore, as your children learn more about navigating using web browsers, their knowledge will produce intelligent and safe surfing. Encourage your children to focus on this chapter and learn all that they can about the World Wide Web!

## Activities Overview

The following chart categorizes each activity to help you to plan the lessons. For example, if you feel that your child would benefit from an arts and crafts activity at a particular time, then choose an activity in the arts and crafts column.

Remember, don't hurry to complete an activity just to have it completed. Your child should work at his or her own pace and really understand the concepts. Create a positive atmosphere while encouraging your child to learn with confidence. To get started, you may decide to plan a fun activity to inspire your child and focus your child's attention on the World Wide Web. If possible, take your child on a tour of a server room at a local business. Explain that all of the computers at businesses are connected to a server, and then the server is connected to other computers that are part of the Internet.

| Activities | Worksheet | Modifiable* | Internet Access | Game | Learning Cards | Slide Show | Arts and Crafts | Answer Key |
|---|---|---|---|---|---|---|---|---|
| 1. World Wide Web Slide Show | | ✔ | | | | ✔ | ✔ | |
| 2. Internet Tutorials | ✔ | ✔ | ✔ | | | | | ✔ |
| 3. URL Worksheet | ✔ | ✔ | | | | | | ✔ |
| 4. URL Cards | ✔ | ✔ | | ✔ | ✔ | | | |
| 5. Web Browsers | ✔ | ✔ | ✔ | | | | | ✔ |
| 6. Internet Dramatization | | ✔ | | ✔ | | ✔ | | |
| 7. Internet Protocol (IP) Address | | | ✔ | | | | | |
| 8. Internet Connection Speeds | | | ✔ | | | | | |
| 9. Switches and Hubs | ✔ | | | | | | | ✔ |
| 10. Quiz | ✔ | | | | | | | ✔ |

* Easily modifiable for younger children

# CD Supplements

The following chart lists all of the CD supplements for this chapter and provides the CD filename, supplement title, and activity number. To make locating and using these supplements faster and easier, it is recommended that you copy all files to your hard drive before beginning the lessons.

| CD Filename | Title | Activity |
|---|---|---|
| 4A | World Wide Web Slide Show | 1 |
| 4B | How the Internet Works Worksheet I | 2 |
| 4C | How the Internet Works Worksheet II | 2 |
| 4D | How the Internet Works Worksheet I Answers | 2 |
| 4E | How the Internet Works Worksheet II Answers | 2 |
| 4F | URL Worksheet | 3 |
| 4G | URL Worksheet Answers | 3 |
| 4H | URL Cards | 4 |
| 4I | Web Browser Worksheet I | 5 |
| 4J | Web Browser Worksheet II | 5 |
| 4K | Web Browser Worksheet I Answers | 5 |
| 4L | Web Browser Worksheet II Answers | 5 |
| 4M | Switches and Hubs Worksheet | 9 |
| 4N | Switches and Hubs Worksheet Answers | 9 |
| 4O | World Wide Web Quiz | 10 |
| 4P | World Wide Web Quiz Answers | 10 |
| 4Q | World Wide Web Vocabulary | Optional |

## Variations for Younger Children

Children are able to navigate the World Wide Web at an early age because computers are readily available to them. Prepare appropriate activities that will allow younger children to explore ideas while giving them sufficient exposure to the World Wide Web. Feel free to modify the activities, for example by removing a step, to meet the needs of your child. Monitor your child's expression to see if he is showing signs of frustration because the activity is too difficult or signs of boredom because the activity is too easy then modify the activity to help him succeed on his individual level. You could even make up your own activities. The following ideas may help.

- Concentrate on a few of the vocabulary terms, instead of teaching all of the skills that are discussed throughout the chapter. You may want to expose your child to all of the skills, but focus on one or two at a time.

- Choose one online tutorial to use and show your child how to navigate using that particular website. While viewing the online tutorial, have him point to the pictures while you read the information to your child, especially if he is still learning to read.

- When explaining web browsers to your children, you may want to show them only one web browser. When teaching about navigation using the web browser, draw a simple house on a piece of paper to represent the home icon on the web browser. Ask your child to find the home icon on the web browser on his computer. Explain to your child that this icon takes you to a specific page called the home page. Continue to draw pictures and teach about other icons on the web browser such as Stop, Refresh, Back, and Forward.

## Internet Safety

In this chapter, some activities require Internet access. Remind your child to think about Internet safety during these activities. You may want to review the Internet safety tips on pages 10–11.

## Fun Decorations

Decorate your home to make this chapter refreshing and fun for everyone. Referring to the room decorations throughout the chapter will help your child think about the World Wide Web and how the Internet really works.

The following are some ideas that might help you with decorations.

- Print the slides from the World Wide Web Slide Show (CD Supplement 4A), staple them to brightly colored construction paper, and display them in your home.

- Dedicate a section of your house to learning about the World Wide Web. Refer to the information located in that area of your home throughout this chapter. Use a banner or letter cutouts to spell out "The World Wide Web," the topic of this chapter. Hang completed work in this area.

- Change the screensaver or the desktop background of your computer to a picture of something, such as a spiderweb, that represents what your child will be learning in this chapter.

- Make a large spiderweb using yarn, markers, or string on a poster board and label it "World Wide Web." Attach four or five pictures of different computers on the web.

- Using a large piece of paper, write a URL that your child uses often, such as a community website, and hang it on the wall. Use this for Activity 4: URL Cards.

- Display posters of the Internet framework or a map of the Internet. Here are a couple examples: www.unc.edu/~unclng/internet-map. gif *or* www.ics.uci.edu/~wscacchi/Tech-EC/EC-EB/Internet-map.gif

## Vocabulary

Review the following terms with your child so that he or she can have a basic understanding of the vocabulary used in this chapter. You could also have your child write the definitions in the World Wide Web Vocabulary worksheet (CD Supplement 4Q).

> **computer:** A programmable machine that processes information.

> **domain name:** Words and dots that represent a specific destination used in URLs.

> **firewall:** A system that restricts the types of services that are accessible on internal systems from the Internet.

> **Internet:** A worldwide network connecting millions of computers.

**IP Address:** Internet Protocol Address. Every computer that connects to the Internet must have a unique number that allows information from it to be routed to another system.

**network:** Computers connected together that share information.

**router:** A device that moves data from one network to another.

**server:** A computer on a network that provides resources for other systems.

**switch/hub:** A device that allows computers to connect with other computers that reside on the same network.

**URL:** Uniform Resource Locator. A complete address on the Internet used to locate a specific page.

**web browser:** Software that allows you to locate and view webpages on the World Wide Web. For example, Mozilla Firefox or Microsoft Internet Explorer.

**World Wide Web:** A network of webpages that can be viewed using a web browser.

# NETS•S Addressed

6. **Technology Operations and Concepts**

   Students demonstrate a sound understanding of technology concepts, systems, and operations. Students:

   a.  understand and use technology systems

   b.  select and use applications effectively and productively

   c.  troubleshoot systems and applications

   d.  transfer current knowledge to the learning of new technologies

# Grades

Your child will have many opportunities to show all he has learned about the World Wide Web in this chapter. Clearly explain throughout the chapter all that is expected of him. Your child's previous knowledge of the World Wide Web may be considered when deciding the assessment method. Determine a way to authentically evaluate your child based on his individual accomplishments and creative abilities. The following are some suggestions that might help you to assess your child.

- Use the answer keys in the various activities to grade the supplements that your child has completed. Base the grades on accuracy or completion. The answer keys can be found on the CD.

- You may want to use the Grade Book located in Appendix A at the back of this book to record your child's assignments and grades.

- Keep a running record of your child's progress to determine comprehension and understanding of the content. Record these observations on paper or in the Grade Book (Appendix A).

- Ask your child to write down the definitions to the vocabulary words in this chapter, using the World Wide Web Vocabulary worksheet (CD Supplement 4Q). This worksheet can be graded.

- Assess your child when he takes the quizzes that are a part of the online tutorials.

- Ask your child to share some interesting trivia that he has learned while using the online tutorials.

- Have your child explain how the Internet works using his own words. Encourage him to use the information learned throughout the chapter.

## Enrichment

Think of ways to expand your child's mind about the World Wide Web and the Internet. The enrichment activities will cause your child to think outside the box and further her understanding about the Internet. Choose one of these extended activities, or come up with your own ideas to encourage your child to go beyond all that she has learned in this chapter.

- Encourage your child to play the tutorials again to learn more about the Internet.

- Show your child some online learning courses she could take or certificates that she could acquire online now or when she is older. Talk to your child about colleges and universities that offer online certificates or degrees.

- Encourage your child to learn about other topics using online tutorials. Research and find some fun and interesting online learning tutorials that spark the interests of your child.

- To motivate higher-level thinking, ask your child to explain how she thinks the Internet may change in the future.

- Have your child research the history of the World Wide Web and explain how it is part of the Internet.

- Have your child research and explain other web browser items not discussed in this chapter, such as History, Bookmarks, Tabs, Help, and Print.

- Have your child type a URL in an address bar, and then modify it to see what happens to the webpage. For example, modify or delete the text after the domain name.

- Have your child research and then write a report explaining the complex parts of the URL such as top-level domain, subdomain, ports, and directories.

- Have your child research online to find out more about IP addresses, such as the difference between public and private IP addresses.

- Have your child think about and plan out ways to increase the Internet connection speed in your home.

## Closure

Promote a sense of accomplishment at the completion of the chapter. Allow a few moments for your child to contemplate all that he has learned about the World Wide Web and the Internet. The following are some suggestions for closure activities.

- Ask, "What have you learned about the World Wide Web?" Encourage your child to share a few interesting facts or trivia learned during this chapter.

- Ask your child to share his favorite activity in this chapter.

Activity **1**

# *World Wide Web Slide Show*

Easy to
Modify for
Younger Kids

## Goal

Your child will watch a slide show and learn about the World Wide Web, the Internet, URLs, and web browsers.

## Materials

- World Wide Web Slide Show (CD Supplement 4A)
- computer
- paper
- colored pencils, markers, or crayons

## Steps

### *1. Prepare*

Open the World Wide Web Slide Show (CD Supplement 4A).
Click Slide Show > View Slide Show when you are ready to begin.

### *2. Learn*

As you advance each slide, have your child read along with you to give your child some basic understanding about the World Wide Web, the Internet, URLs, and web browsers.

### *3. Review*

Show the slide show again and have your child recall the definitions before they appear on the screen. Your child could advance the slides during the multimedia presentation.

## 4. Draw

Have your child use colored pencils, markers, or crayons to draw a picture showing how the Internet works.

**Tip**
Check out a book from your local library about the World Wide Web and the Internet for your child to read.

Activity **2**

# Internet Tutorials

Easy to
Modify for
Younger Kids

## Goal

Your child will use an online tutorial to learn about the Internet and complete a worksheet.

## Materials

- How the Internet Works Worksheet I or II (CD Supplement 4B or 4C)
- How the Internet Works Worksheet I or II Answers (CD Supplement 4D or 4E)
- computer with Internet access
- pencil

## Steps

### 1. Prepare

Listed below are several online tutorials. Choose the sites that will be the best for your child's age and abilities. Become familiar with the websites ahead of time, so you will know how to navigate the sites. Please note that each tutorial explains the Internet in a different way, so it is beneficial to allow your child to use more than one tutorial to maximize her learning experience.

**The Animated Internet: How the Web Works:**
www.learnthenet.com/english/section/www.html

**BrainPop (account required):** www.brainpop.com/technology/seeall/

**How Stuff Works:**
http://computer.howstuffworks.com/internet-infrastructure.htm

**Internet Explorer 5 in the Classroom:** www.actden.com/IE5/

**Looney Tunes Teach the Internet:**
http://looneytunes2.warnerbros.com/ltti/

**Networks Windows NT:** www.actden.com/skills2k/net.htm

**The World Wide Web Microsoft Internet Explorer:**
www.actden.com/skills2k/www.htm

## 2. Tutorial

Allow your child to view the online tutorials, or have her complete the sections of the tutorials that you want to focus on with your child. Your child may need to view the tutorials more than once to completely understand the information.

## 3. Worksheet

Decide which How the Internet Works Worksheet (I or II) will best meet the needs of your child. Print out the appropriate worksheet (CD Supplement 4B or 4C).

Explain the directions at the top of the worksheet and give your child sufficient time to complete it. If needed, allow your child to watch the tutorials again or choose a different tutorial for her to find the information she needs to complete the worksheet.

If your child is completing the How the Internet Works Worksheet II, encourage her to write the description of the terms using her own words.

## 4. Check

Use How the Internet Works Worksheet I or II Answers (CD Supplement 4D or 4E) to check your child's work. Go over any missed items.

**Tips**
While reading the online tutorial, point out specific terms and ask your child what that term means. This will help your child think about the terms and how to come up with a definition. Print out some of the basic facts about the Internet from one of the tutorials and give it to your child to read.

Activity **3**

# URL Worksheet

## Goal

Your child will complete a URL worksheet to learn about the parts of a website address.

## Materials

- URL Worksheet (CD Supplement 4F)
- URL Worksheet Answers (CD Supplement 4G)
- computer with Internet access
- pencil

## Steps

### 1. URL

Open a web browser and have your child type a URL in the address bar. Discuss the different parts of the website address including document name, separators, subdirectory name, domain name, and protocol.

### 2. Worksheet

Have your child use the word list to fill in the boxes with the appropriate term on the URL Worksheet (CD Supplement 4F). If needed, allow your child to view the slide show again or watch a tutorial to complete the worksheet.

### 3. Check

Use the URL Worksheet Answers (CD Supplement 4G) to check your child's work. Go over any missed items.

**Tips**
For fun, have your child find URLs on cereal boxes, toys, games, or other items and talk about the different parts of the URL. URLs are more complicated than what has been presented in this activity; have your child research hosts, top-level domain, FQDN (Fully Qualified Domain Name), and other terms.

Activity **4**

# URL Cards

Easy to
Modify for
Younger Kids

## Goal

Your child will review the parts of a URL and then play a matching game.

## Materials

- URL Cards (CD Supplement 4H)
- scissors
- paper
- markers
- tape
- yarn or string

## Steps

### 1. Prepare

Print and then cut out the URL Cards (CD Supplement 4H). Glue them to construction paper for added durability.

### 2. Review

Before you begin, you may want to review the parts of the URL with your child.

### 3. Write

Write a website address on a large piece of paper using large letters and hang it on the wall. If you need more space, attach two or more pieces of paper together with tape. Tape the URL cards close to the address, but in random places on the wall.

## 4. *Play*

Have your child tape yarn or string onto the URL card and then tape it to the correct place on the website address. Write another URL on different paper and have your child play again.

**Tips**
For more information on URLs, have your child find the meaning of different protocols: http, https, ftp, and sftp. Children could also research the meaning of different top-level domain names such as .com, .net, .edu, .org, .gov and country codes such as .in, .cn, .kr, or .ru. For fun, try www.google.cn.

Activity 5

# Web Browsers

Easy to
Modify for
Younger Kids

## Goal

Your child will practice some basic navigation techniques using a web browser and then complete a worksheet.

## Materials

- Web Browser Worksheet I or II (CD Supplement 4I or 4J)
- Web Browser Worksheet I or II Answers (CD Supplement 4K or 4L)
- computer with Internet access
- Web browser (Microsoft Internet Explorer or Mozilla Firefox)
- pencil

## Steps

### 1. View

Allow your child to view a web browser at the computer while explaining how to navigate using the navigation toolbar and standard icons.

### 2. Practice

Practice some basic navigation techniques by calling out icons such as Back, Forward, Refresh, Home, and Stop as your child clicks on the correct icon on the browser.

### 3. Worksheet

Depending upon the age and ability of your child, have your child complete either Web Browser Worksheet I or II (CD Supplement 4I or 4J). Print the appropriate worksheet. Explain the instructions that are written on the worksheet and answer and questions. Give your child enough time to complete the worksheet.

## 4. Check

Use the Web Browser I or II Answers (CD Supplement 4K or 4L) to grade your child's work. Go over any missed items.

**Tips**

Show your child the differences among various browsers (e.g., Microsoft Internet Explorer or Mozilla Firefox). You may want to show your child how to create a home page or a bookmark for his favorite website. It may be helpful to show your child how to add and remove buttons to the web browser.

Activity **6**

# Internet Dramatization

## Goal

Your child will create a visual representation of the Internet using yarn and boxes.

## Materials

- yarn or string
- four small boxes or cartons
- tape
- paper
- colored pencils, markers, or crayons

## Steps

### 1. Question

Ask your child, "When you go online to a website, how does that information get onto your computer screen?" Allow your child to share her answer or write it on a piece of paper. It may be fun to find out your child's ideas of how the Internet works, which also gives you an idea of her level of understanding.

### 2. Network

Place the boxes or cartons around a room. Have your child stretch yarn across the room to make a web by taping the yarn to the boxes. Explain to your child that information passes through wires from one computer to another. The yarn is a representation of the wires while the boxes are like computers. The information passes very quickly over the wires to computers. This is a very simple explanation of how computers talk to each other in a network.

### 3. Internet

Have your child act as if she is a byte of data going from one box to the other. Tell her to run as fast as she can for 30 seconds to and from the boxes because she is transmitting messages from one computer to another. Then have her sit while you share that the Internet is the largest network of all. It is composed of computers connecting to one another via Internet Service Providers (ISPs). ISPs have numerous modems and routers (modem banks) that allow a home or business computer to communicate on the larger Internet pathway. ISPs connect to each other via national and international communication lines, most of which are made of fiber optics. These lines comprise the backbone of the Internet. They transmit information at extremely high speeds, much faster than any computer is capable of sending or receiving information.

### 4. Multiple Networks

Allow your child to create an entirely new network in another room of your home. Remember to connect the two networks (rooms) using wire (yarn). Share that the Internet consists of many independent networks connected via routers. A router takes the information from one network and transmits it to another network. In that way, a computer network in New York can route messages to a completely different network in Tokyo, Japan. Network engineers work with routers to make communication between networks as efficient as possible.

### 5. Draw

After completing this dramatization, have your child use colored pencils, markers, or crayons to draw a picture showing how the Internet works. You may want to compare this drawing to the picture she made in Activity 1: World Wide Web Slide Show. Have her use her drawing and tell you again in her own words how the Internet works.

**Tips**
Create signs that say *computer*, *wires*, and *byte*, then attach them to the boxes, yarn, and your child during the dramatization. For added fun, be creative and allow your child to create a huge World Wide Web in your home using lots of yarn.

Activity **7**

# Internet Protocol (IP) Address

## Goal

Your child will determine the IP address for his computer.

## Materials

- computer with Internet access
- paper and pencil

## Steps

### 1. IP Address

Everything that connects to the Internet must have an IP address. Explain that just as you have a mailing address for your home, your computer has an IP address so it can connect to the Internet. The Internet Protocol is a set of rules used for communicating on the Internet.

### 2. Type

To find the IP address of your computer, go to a command prompt on your computer.

**For Windows 2000, XP, or Vista**

Go to: Start > Programs > Accessories > Command Prompt
Type: ipconfig
Press: Enter key

**For Linux**

Go to: a terminal window
Type: ifconfig | grep inet
Press: Enter key

**For Macintosh**

Go to: Applications > Utilities > Terminal
Type: ifconfig | grep inet
Press: Return key

## 3. Record

Have your child write down your IP address. You need to find the list of numbers that corresponds to your current network. The IP address is the set of numbers with three periods after the word "inet." You will see slight variations in how the IP address is listed, depending on your operating system. You should see something similiar to this at the command prompt:

```
hpoteete$ ifconfig | grep inet
    inet6 ::1 prefixlen 128
    inet6 fe80::1%lo0 prefixlen 64 scopeid 0x1
    inet 127.0.0.1 netmask 0xff000000
    inet6 fe80::fa1e:dfff:fed6:ddb%en1 prefixlen 64 scopeid 0x5
    inet 192.168.0.78 netmask 0xffffff00 broadcast 192.168.0.255
```

In this example, the IP address that corresponds to the network is 192.168.0.78.

Activity 8

# Internet Connection Speeds

## Goal

Your child will use a website to determine her Internet connection speed and record the results.

## Materials

- computer with Internet access
- paper and pencil

## Steps

### 1. Test Speed

Have your child find out the download and upload speed of your Internet connection in your home by using an online speed test such as www.speakeasy.net/speedtest/ *or* www.speedtest.net.

### 2. Record

Instruct your child to write the results of the speed test on a piece of paper.

### 3. Test Again

Sometimes your connection speed changes at different times during the day or night. It will also change depending on how many computers are connected to the network and are actively transmitting information (network congestion). Have your child find out the best time to surf the web using your home computer by testing the connection speed at different times throughout the day.

### 4. Best Time

Ask your child to write the time of day and the results of the speed tests on a piece of paper. The higher the number, the faster the connection. Have her circle the best time of day to surf the web on your computer, which will be the fastest connection speed.

Activity 9

# Switches and Hubs

## Goal

Your child will learn about switches and hubs and complete a worksheet.

## Materials

- Switches and Hubs Worksheet (CD Supplement 4M)
- Switches and Hubs Worksheet Answers (CD Supplement 4N)
- a computer switch or hub (optional)
- Ethernet cable (optional)

## Steps

### 1. Show

Show your child an actual switch or a hub or a picture of one. You could show him one that you use in your home or go to a computer parts store to show him the device.

Switches and hubs have ports. The ports are the small network jacks into which you plug your computer network cable. If you have an Ethernet cable, you could also show him how the cable plugs into the port. Switches and hubs connect computers together, creating Local Area Networks (LANs). Remind your child that the Internet is the largest network of all.

### 2. Worksheet

Have your child complete the Switches and Hubs Worksheet (CD Supplement 4M) to learn more about the differences in these devices.

## 3. Check

Use the Switches and Hubs Worksheet Answers (CD Supplement 4N) to grade your child's work. Go over any missed items with your child.

**Tips**

Allow your child to help you pick out a switch if you need one for your home network. Both switches and hubs are built to transmit data at specific speeds. Be sure to pick a switch or a hub that has a speed rating sufficient for your network—faster is better. Also, pick one that has enough ports for every computer, printer, router, wireless access point, or other network device that you wish to connect to your new Local Area Network (LAN).

Usually, switches and hubs are rated by megabits per second or Mbps (notice the capital "M" for Mega, and the lowercase "b" for bit. A lowercase "m" would represent milli, and an uppercase "B" would represent byte.) Per second is abbreviated "ps." It is normal to see network units rated as 10/100/1,000 Mbps.

Activity **10**

# Quiz

## Goal

Your child will take a quiz on the information she has learned about the World Wide Web and the Internet.

## Materials

- World Wide Web Quiz (CD Supplement 4O)
- World Wide Web Quiz Answers (CD Supplement 4P)
- pencil
- computer with Internet access (optional)

## Steps

### 1. Review

Use any worksheets, drawings, and notes from the activities in this chapter to review the information on the World Wide Web and the Internet.

### 2. Quiz

Print the World Wide Web Quiz (CD Supplement 4O). Explain the instructions, answer any questions, and provide your child with enough time to complete the quiz.

### 3. Check

Use the World Wide Web Quiz Answers (CD Supplement 4P) to grade your child's work. The answers given are only samples because actual answers will vary greatly. Go over any missed questions with your child.

**Tip**
Allow your child to use her computer to find the answers during the quiz.

## Chapter 5

# Word Processing

## Objective

Children will learn basic word processing skills using tutorials, worksheets, checklists, and a word processor.

## Purpose

Show your child that this chapter has value for her so that she will be committed to learning. Discuss the importance of knowing how to create word processing documents for school assignments. Word processing skills are the basis for many jobs such as computer graphics artists and administrators. There will be many opportunities to create word processing documents such as making a garage sale sign, typing a letter, sending an e-mail, or writing a story. Therefore, encourage your child to really focus on this chapter and learn all that she can about word processing!

## Activities Overview

The activities in this chapter offer many ways to learn and increase skills using a word processor. Carefully consider which activities and websites will benefit your child depending on his age, abilities, and learning styles. The following chart categorizes each activity to help you to plan the lessons. Some children may be able to complete all of the activities, while others would benefit by focusing more time on a few key activities. Certain children may require a more structured environment, whereas a self-motivated child could be given more freedom to work.

Create a positive atmosphere while encouraging your child to learn with confidence. To get started, you may decide to plan a fun activity to inspire your child and focus his attention on word processing. You could use a word processing program to write a special letter to your child telling him a story of something cute that he did when he was younger. This letter may prompt your child to focus on word processing, and he will be more interested and ready to learn.

| Activities | Worksheet | Modifiable* | Internet Access | Game | Learning Cards | Slide Show | Arts and Crafts | Answer Key |
|---|---|---|---|---|---|---|---|---|
| 1. Word Processing Icons | ✔ | | | | | | | ✔ |
| 2. Word Processing Tutorials | | ✔ | ✔ | | | | | |
| 3. Skills Checklist | ✔ | ✔ | | | | | | |
| 4. Documents | ✔ | ✔ | | ✔ | | | | |
| 5. Poem | | ✔ | ✔ | | | | | |
| 6. Recipe | | | ✔ | | | | | |
| 7. Greeting Card | | | ✔ | | | | ✔ | |
| 8. Word Search | | | | ✔ | | | | |
| 9. Newsletter | | | | ✔ | | | | |
| 10. Quiz | ✔ | | | | | | | ✔ |

* Easily modifiable for younger children

# CD Supplements

The following chart lists all of the CD supplements for this chapter and provides the CD filename, supplement title, and activity number. To make locating and using these supplements faster and easier, it is recommended that you copy all files to your hard drive before beginning the lessons.

| CD Filename | Title | Activity |
|---|---|---|
| 5A | Word Icon Worksheet | 1 |
| 5B | Writer Icon Worksheet | 1 |
| 5C | Word Icon Worksheet Answers | 1 |
| 5D | Writer Icon Worksheet Answers | 1 |
| 5E | Skills Checklist I | 3 |
| 5F | Skills Checklist II | 3 |
| 5G | Word Processing Cards | 4 |
| 5H | Word Processing Quiz I | 10 |
| 5I | Word Processing Quiz II | 10 |
| 5J | Word Processing Quiz I Answers | 10 |
| 5K | Word Processing Vocabulary | Optional |

# Variations for Younger Children

Children are able to create and explore word processors at an early age. Prepare appropriate activities that will allow younger children to explore ideas while giving them sufficient exposure to word processing. Feel free to modify the activities, such as removing a step, to meet the needs of your child. Monitor your child's expression to see if she is showing signs of frustration because the activity is too difficult or signs of boredom because the activity is too easy then modify the activity to help her succeed on his individual level. You could even make up your own activities. The following ideas may help.

- Concentrate on a few of the word processing skills, instead of teaching all of the skills that are discussed throughout the chapter.

- Use a very simple word processor such as Notepad or gedit to teach basic word processing skills. Use a paint program such as Microsoft Paint or gpaint to teach basic drawing and mouse actions.

## Internet Safety

In this chapter, some activities require Internet access. Remind your child to think about Internet safety during these activities. You may want to review the Internet safety tips on pages 10–11.

## Fun Decorations

Do something different at your house for this chapter by creating an environment that will excite your child about word processing. Decorations can generate enthusiasm as well as provide another opportunity to teach your child about word processing. Be inventive as you plan the room decorations, and remember to have fun! The following are some ideas that might help you with decorations.

- Dedicate a section of your house to learning about word processing. Refer to the information located in that area of your home throughout this chapter. Use a banner or letter cutouts to spell out "Word Processing," the topic of this chapter. Hang completed work in this area.

- Change the screensaver or the desktop background of your computer to a graphic that represents something that your child will be learning in this chapter, for example, a keyboard or a picture of a computer.

- Make up a theme for the entire chapter such as plants or the solar system. As you and your child work through each activity, incorporate facts from your theme so your child is learning about another topic while learning word processing skills.

## Vocabulary

Review the following terms with your child so that he or she can have a basic understanding of the vocabulary used in this chapter. You could also have your child write the definitions in the Word Processing Vocabulary worksheet (CD Supplement 5K).

**bold:** Makes the highlighted text boldface.

**center:** Places highlighted text or objects in the middle of the document.

**copy:** Duplicates the highlighted text.

**document:** A file produced or edited by a word processor.

**icon:** A small picture that represents a menu command.

**justified text:** Text that is aligned evenly between the left and right margins.

**save:** Keeps a copy of the document on your computer.

**spell check:** Ensures words are spelled correctly.

**text:** Typed words.

**underline:** Puts a line under the highlighted text.

**undo:** Removes the last word processing task that you did.

**word processor:** A computer program used to create and edit documents.

# NETS•S Addressed

1.  **Creativity and Innovation**

    Students demonstrate creative thinking, construct knowledge, and develop innovative products and processes using technology. Students:

    a.  apply existing knowledge to generate new ideas, products, or processes

    b.  create original works as a means of personal or group expression

    c.  use models and simulations to explore complex systems and issues

    d.  identify trends and forecast possibilities

# Grades

Think of the best way to determine your child's comprehension of this chapter on word processing skills. This is your child's opportunity to demonstrate her individual understanding. Throughout each activity, evaluate your child while she works. When deciding on the type of assessment, consider her age and abilities and give clear expectations so that she understands all that is expected of her and as a result she can be successful. The following are some suggestions that might help you to assess your child.

- Use the answer keys in the various activities to grade the supplements that your child completed. Base the grades on accuracy or completion. The answer keys can be found on the CD. You may want to use the Grade Book located in Appendix A at the back of this book to record your child's assignments and grades.

- Keep a running record of your child's progress to determine comprehension and understanding of the content. Record these observations on paper or in the Grade Book (Appendix A).

- Ask your child to write down the definitions to the vocabulary words in this chapter using the Word Processing Vocabulary worksheet (CD Supplement 5K). Have your child print some of the word processing documents and turn them in to you for a grade. Assess your child when she takes the quizzes that are a part of the online tutorials.

# Enrichment

Provide opportunities for your child to build upon the word processing skills learned in this chapter. Choose one of these enrichment activities, or plan your own that will motivate and move your child to the next level in his word processing skills.

- Have your child make a list of some of the word processing shortcuts such as Ctrl+C (copy) and Ctrl+V (paste) and display them next to the computer so that he can use them when typing.

- Encourage your child to practice different word processing skills that were not discussed in this chapter. Encourage your child to play the tutorials again to practice as well as learn more word processing skills.

- Have your child try different types of word processors and explain what he likes about each one. Your child could research the differences between Microsoft Word and OpenOffice Writer and list the advantages and disadvantages of these word processors.

- Have your child open all of the toolbars in the word processing document and see how much space he has left to write. Then have him close all of the toolbars, except the toolbars you would like to keep on the screen.

- Assign your child a task of writing a weekly or monthly newsletter for your family events.

- Have your child research the first word processors and how they differ from current word processors.

- Ask your child to explain the similarities and differences among word processing, spreadsheet, and slide show programs.

- Teach your child how to make backups of his work by saving his files to another computer on your home network, or by using a CD, USB drive, or another type of backup. Teach him about the importance of keeping an extra copy of important work just in case something happens to his original data.

## Closure

After all the activities in the chapter have been completed, allow a few moments for your child to think about all she has learned concerning word processing. This allows your child to process and reflect upon all that she has learned about icons, word processors, and creating documents. The following are some suggestions for closure activities.

- Ask your child, "What have you learned about word processing?" Encourage your child to share a few interesting facts or trivia that she has learned during this chapter.

- Ask your child to write a letter to you describing a few of the things that she has learned about word processing.

Activity **1**

# Word Processing Icons

## Goal

Your child will learn the meaning of 10 basic icons from the standard and formatting toolbars.

## Materials

- Word Icon Worksheet (CD Supplement 5A)
- Writer Icon Worksheet (CD Supplement 5B)
- Word Icon Worksheet Answers (CD Supplement 5C)
- Writer Icon Worksheet Answers (CD Supplement 5D)
- computer
- pencil
- word processor (Microsoft Word or OpenOffice Writer)

## Steps

### 1. Prepare

Decide which word processor you would like to use for this activity. If you need a word processing program, OpenOffice.org (www.openoffice.org) offers Write, a free program that can be downloaded and installed on your computer.

### 2. Learn

Depending on the word processor you've chosen, give your child either the Word or Writer Icons Worksheet (CD Supplement 5A or 5B). Have your child open and use the program to complete the worksheet by writing the description of each labeled icon in the space provided. The icons include Save, Print, Spell Check, Copy, Bold, Undo, Underline, Center, Bullets, and Highlight. Explain that icons are symbols that do something when you click on them.

## 3. Check

Use the Word or Writer Icon Worksheet Answers (CD Supplement 5C or 5D) to check your child's work. Go over any missed items.

## 4. Explore

Give your child a few minutes to explore the word processor by clicking other icons to find out what they do. You may want to have your child draw five more icons and then write down the purpose of these icons.

**Tips**

Show your child that if he hovers over an icon with the mouse, he will see a short description of what it does. Warn him to be careful not to click on an icon accidentally because it could do something that he doesn't want it to do. For example, he should not click the Print icon before he's ready, because it will print the document.

Activity **2**

# Word Processing Tutorials

Easy to
Modify for
Younger Kids

## Goal

Your child will use an online tutorial to learn about word processing.

## Materials

- computer with Internet access
- paper and pencil
- word processor (Microsoft Word or OpenOffice Writer)

## Steps

### 1. Prepare

Listed below are several online tutorials for Microsoft Word and
OpenOffice Writer. Choose the one that will be the best for your
child's age and abilities. Become familiar with the website ahead of
time, so you will know how to navigate the site. Your child could use
more than one tutorial.

**Microsoft Word Tutorials**

> **Internet4Classrooms—Microsoft Word Modules:**
> www.internet4classrooms.com/on-line_word.htm

> **Microsoft Office Online: Get to Know Word:** http://office.microsoft.com/
> training/training.aspx?AssetID=RC100140951033

> **Word training course—Microsoft Office online training videos:**
> www.free-training-tutorial.com/msWord2007-formattingText.html

**OpenOffice Writer Tutorials**

> **Introduction to OpenOffice Writer 2.0:**
> www.ischool.utexas.edu/technology/tutorials/office/oowriter/

> **OpenOffice.org Writer In Pictures:** http://inpics.net/writer.html

> **Tutorials for OpenOffice: Word Processing (Writer):**
> www.tutorialsforopenoffice.org/category_index/wordprocessing.html

## 2. Tutorial

Allow your child to complete the online tutorial or just have her complete the sections that you want to focus on with her. Have your child take notes from the site or complete any questions or quizzes during the tutorial.

## 3. Share

Have your child share some interesting facts she has learned while viewing the tutorial. Give her a few minutes to try some of the things she has learned.

**Tips**
Write the word processing skills on a piece of paper to clearly show which skills you want your child to focus on during the tutorial. You may want to have your child try new word processing concepts when they are taught during the tutorial.

Activity **3**

# Skills Checklist

Easy to Modify for Younger Kids

## Goal

Your child will learn and practice various word processing skills and complete a checklist.

## Materials and Equipment

- Skills Checklist I or II (CD Supplement 5E and 5F)
- pencil
- computer
- word processor (Microsoft Word or OpenOffice Writer)

## Steps

### 1. Show

Show your child how to perform several word processing functions, such as change the font, insert bullets, or bold text. It may help to have your child sit with hands folded watching until you finish explaining, or your child might keep working and miss information that he needs.

### 2. Practice

Allow your child to practice the new skills using the computer. For example, if you show him how to make a bulleted list, he could type the words "dog," "cat," and "mouse," pressing Enter after each word. Next, have your child select these words and click the Bullets icon. Show your child as many word processing functions as you feel he is able to learn.

## 3. Checklist

Have your child use the Skills Checklist I or II (CD Supplement 5E or 5F) as a guide for practicing word processing skills. Once the skill is mastered, place a check in the box next to the skill. Depending on your child's abilities, consider assigning only a section of the items on the checklist.

**Tips**

Teach your child how to use the Undo icon first. Your child will appreciate the ease with which he can undo his mistakes.

It may be easier to have younger children type in all caps or in all lowercase instead of using the shift keys. For younger children, mastering a few of the word processing skills may be more important than knowing how to do every skill on the checklist.

Activity 4

# *Documents*

Easy to Modify for Younger Kids

## Goal

Your child will type, modify, save, close, and then open a document.

## Materials

- Word Processing Cards (CD Supplement 5G)
- scissors
- computer
- word processor (Microsoft Word or OpenOffice Writer)

## Steps

### 1. Type

Open the word processor. Have your child type her name, address, and birthday. Then she should learn to save her document. Have her click File, select Save, type a filename, and click Save.

### 2. Modify

Have your child modify her text by changing the font size, color, style, and anything else that she would like to try. She could use her favorite color. Your child should then save her document again. Remind her to save often! Your child should close her document and the word processor.

### 3. Open

Have your child open this file. This is to make sure that she knows how to save and then open the file that she has created.

## *4. Practice*

Hold up one of the Word Processing Cards (CD Supplement 5G), and your child should do what the card says. For example, if the card says "Make a new file," then your child should create a new file.

**Tips**
Show your child the different ways to open the word processor. Depending on the operating system and version installed on your computer, there are different ways to open the word processor, such as using the start menu or applications folder, clicking a shortcut on the desktop, or clicking a shortcut on the toolbar. You may want to show her how to create a new folder on the computer and save all of her work for this chapter in this folder.

Activity **5**

# Poem

Easy to Modify for Younger Kids

## Goal

Your child will read poems online, then type and center a poem using a word processor.

## Materials

- computer with Internet access
- books with poetry
- word processor (Microsoft Word or OpenOffice Writer)
- printer
- paper for printer

## Steps

### 1. Read

Allow your child to read several poems online from one of the sites listed below, or he could read poetry from a favorite book. Before this activity, determine which websites will be the most appropriate for your child to use.

**Apples4TheTeacher:** www.apples4theteacher.com/poetry.html

**Famous Poetry Online:** www.poetry-online.org

### 2. Type

Have your child write a poem using a word processor. Go over any specific details that you want to be included in the poem, or the type of poem you want your child to create.

### 3. Center

Teach your child how to highlight or select the entire poem and center it on the page by clicking the Center icon.

## 4. Print

Print the poem and display it.

> **Tips**
> Have your child insert a graphic or modify the text in different ways for extra practice. For fun, enter your child's poem into a poetry contest.

Activity **6**

# Recipe

## Goal

Your child will type a recipe and then create bulleted and numbered lists.

## Materials

- computer with Internet access
- word processor (Microsoft Word or OpenOffice Writer)
- printer
- paper for printer

## Steps

### 1. Online

Choose one of the websites below to search for a recipe to use in this activity or use a family favorite.

**Children's Recipes—Cooking with Kids:** www.childrensrecipes.com

**Disney FamilyFun: Recipes:** http://familyfun.go.com/recipes/

### 2. Type

Have your child type the ingredients and steps to her favorite recipe using a word processor. Alternately, she could make up a recipe.

### 3. Bullets

Teach your child how to select the recipe ingredients and click the Bullets icon to make a bulleted list.

### 4. Numbering

Show your child how to select her recipe steps and click the Numbering icon to create a numbered list automatically.

## 5. *Eat*

For fun, print the recipe and then have your child follow the recipe to make the dish. Enjoy—and good luck, especially if your child made up the recipe!

**Tip**
If you need help showing your child how to create bulleted or numbered lists, use the help feature on your word processor.

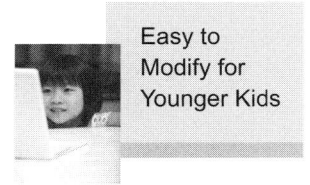

Easy to
Modify for
Younger Kids

Activity 7

# Greeting Card

## Goal

Your child will create a greeting card that includes a graphic.

## Materials

- computer
- word processor (Microsoft Word or OpenOffice Writer)
- printer
- paper for printer
- construction paper
- stapler, tape, or glue
- markers, crayons, glitter, stickers, paint (optional)

## Steps

### 1. Type

Have your child type "Happy Birthday," "Get Well Soon," or another type of greeting to create a card to give to someone. Your child could modify the text size, color, and style.

### 2. Graphic or Picture

Next, your child should insert a graphic or a picture into the document. Show your child how to move the graphic and increase and decrease the size of the graphic. There are many ways to modify the graphic, so allow your child to explore the different options available on your word processor. For example, click on the graphic so a box appears around the graphic. Click and drag on the corners or sides to enlarge or shrink the graphic. For a list of more ways to change the graphic, right click directly on the graphic.

### 3. Border

Show your child how to insert a page border on the document.

### 4. Print

Have your child print the document then attach it to a piece of construction paper using glue, tape, or a stapler to make the front of the card. Then staple another piece of construction paper to it, making the inside of the card. Your child could type or write a special message on the inside of the card.

### 5. Decorate

Encourage your child to use markers, crayons, glitter, stickers, paint, or other creative materials to make his card unique.

**Tip**
If you need help showing your child how to insert or modify the graphic, or how to insert a border, use the help feature on your word processor.

Activity 8

# Word Search

## Goal

Your child will create a word search by creating a table using a word processor.

## Materials

- computer
- word processor (Microsoft Word or OpenOffice Writer)
- printer
- paper for printer

## Steps

### 1. Prepare

Have your child type five words on a certain topic to be used in a word search, such as five types of fruits or five animals. This will be her word list.

### 2. Table

Show your child how to insert a table using the word processor. Have her create a table that has 20 columns and 10 rows.

### 3. Type

Have your child type her words into the table forward, backward, upside down, or diagonally using all caps by typing one letter into each square. See the following example.

| | | | | | | | | S | | | | | | | | | |
|---|---|---|---|---|---|---|---|---|---|---|---|---|---|---|---|---|---|
| | | | | A | P | P | L | E | | | | | O | | | | |
| | | | N | | | | P | | | | | R | | | | | |
| | | A | | | | | A | | | | | A | | | | | |
| | N | | | | | | R | | | | | N | | | | | |
| | A | | | | | | G | | | | | G | | | | | |
| B | | | | | | | | | | | P | E | A | R | | | |

## 4. Fill

Then have your child fill in the remaining squares with random letters and center the letters inside the table. Your child could type a title at the top of the document.

## 5. Print

Have your child print the word search and give it to a friend to try. The friend should try to find the words in the word list that are hidden in the puzzle and circle them.

**Tips**
Your child could remove the borders of the tables, so that just the letters are showing without the lines (this is an advanced skill). If you need help showing your child how to create or modify tables, use the help feature on your word processor.

Activity **9**

# Newsletter

## Goal

Your child will create a newsletter using many word processing skills.

## Materials

- sample newsletters or newspapers
- computer with Internet access
- pencil and paper
- word processor
- printer
- paper for printer

## Steps

### 1. View

Allow your child to look at a few sample newsletters or an old newspaper to get a few ideas of what to include and how to design his newsletter. He could also go online and read the local newspaper.

### 2. Design

Your child should draw a rough layout on a piece of paper of all that he would like to include in his newsletter, such as a title, topics, announcements, the weather, birthdays, holidays, or anything else that interests him. Be sure to give him any guidelines that you want him to follow when creating his newsletter.

### 3. Type

Have your child write at least one article for the newsletter using a word processor then insert a title, the date, graphics, and other items. Allow him to incorporate some of the word processing skills learned in this chapter, such as inserting a picture, creating a bulleted or numbered list, or inserting a table.

## 4. Justified

Show your child how to create justified text for his newsletter article.

## 5. Print

Have your child print his newsletter and display it in your home.

**Tips**
Encourage your child to work at his individual level of understanding when creating the article or articles for this newsletter. If your child seems to show interest in publishing, then further his skills by using templates found online or use the templates integrated in your word processor to create a more complex newsletter.

Activity **10**

# *Quiz*

## Goal

Your child will review word processing concepts and then take a quiz.

## Materials

- Word Processing Quiz I or II (CD Supplement 5H or 5I)
- Word Processing Quiz I Answers (CD Supplement 5J)
- word processor (Microsoft Word or OpenOffice Writer)
- pencil

## Steps

### 1. Review

Have your child open the word processor and then ask her to show you how to do a particular word processing skill. For example, tell your child: "Type a list of four of your favorite foods, and then make it a numbered list." Your child should make a numbered list of four foods. Continue to call out word processing tasks to your child, such as indent, spell check, center, copy and paste, print preview, insert a graphic, and more. Refer to the checklists from Activity 3: Skills Checklist (CD Supplements 5E and 5F) for more ideas.

### 2. Quiz

Decide which Word Processing Quiz (I or II) will best meet the needs of your child. Explain the instructions at the top of the quiz. Give your child enough time to complete the quiz.

### 3. Check

Use the Word Processing Quiz I Answers (CD Supplement 5J) to grade your child's work. The answers vary for Quiz II depending on the type of word processor used. To check Quiz II, have your child read the words she has written on the quiz as she shows you the menu items she would click on the word processor. Then she could point to the icon on the word processor and make sure it matches the picture that she has drawn for each number. Go over any missed questions with your child.

## Chapter 6

# Internet Research

## Objective

Children will learn to research on the Internet using a variety of methods and fun topics and then create a slide presentation using the information that they gathered during the research activities.

## Purpose

This chapter on Internet research is very important in the Information Age because children need to learn how to locate information online and narrow their focus to locate viable and appropriate resources. It is important that your children understand the purpose of this material and make the content their own. Processing this information to create a slide show displays creativity and your child's individuality. Your children should feel a sense of achievement when they create their own projects using individual research and ideas. Children will become motivated to research more often because it is quick and simple to find the answer to questions when searching online. This chapter will teach your children how to learn new things about fun topics such as ocean animals, weather, natural hazards, and birds with the World Wide Web at their fingertips.

## Activities Overview

This chapter will teach your child to research online through a variety of fun learning activities. Carefully consider which activities will benefit your child depending on his or her age, abilities, and learning styles. The following chart categorizes each activity to help you to plan the lessons. Some children may be able to complete all of them, while others would benefit by focusing more time on a few key activities. Certain children may require a more structured environment, whereas a self-motivated child could be given more freedom.

Remember, don't hurry to complete an activity just to have it completed; your child should work at his or her own pace and really understand the concepts. You may want to repeat an activity or allow your child more time on a certain activity such as Activity 9: Create a Slide. Create a positive atmosphere while encouraging your child to learn with confidence. To get started, you may decide to plan a fun activity to inspire your child and focus your child's attention on Internet research.

| Activities | Worksheet | Modifiable* | Internet Access | Game | Learning Cards | Slide Show | Arts and Crafts | Answer Key |
|---|---|---|---|---|---|---|---|---|
| 1. Search Engines | | | ✔ | | | | | |
| 2. Bird Research | ✔ | | ✔ | | | | | |
| 3. Ocean Animal Research | ✔ | | ✔ | | | | | |
| 4. Natural Hazard Cards | ✔ | ✔ | ✔ | ✔ | ✔ | | | |
| 5. Natural Hazards Research | ✔ | | ✔ | | | | | |
| 6. Weather Bear | ✔ | ✔ | ✔ | | | | ✔ | |
| 7. Weather Chart | ✔ | | ✔ | | | | | |
| 8. Choose a Topic | ✔ | | ✔ | | | | | |
| 9. Create a Slide | ✔ | ✔ | | | | ✔ | | |
| 10. Slide Presentation | ✔ | ✔ | | | | ✔ | | |

* Easily modifiable for younger children

# CD Supplements

The following chart lists all of the CD supplements for this chapter and provides the CD filename, supplement title, and activity number. To make locating and using these supplements faster and easier, it is recommended that you copy all files to your hard drive before beginning the lessons.

| CD Filename | Title | Activity |
|---|---|---|
| 6A | Bird Worksheet | 2 |
| 6B | Ocean Animal Worksheet | 3 |
| 6C | Natural Hazard Cards | 4 |
| 6D | Natural Hazards Worksheet I | 5 |
| 6E | Natural Hazards Worksheet II | 5 |
| 6F | Weather Bear Worksheet | 6 |
| 6G | Weather Chart | 7 |
| 6H | Research Worksheet I | 8 |
| 6I | Research Worksheet II | 8 |
| 6J | Slide Worksheet | 9 |
| 6K | Sample Slides | 9 |
| 6L | Presentation Grading Sheet | 10 |
| 6M | Internet Research Vocabulary | Optional |

# Variations for Younger Children

Even though younger children may not be able to understand the reason for reading and processing the information, this chapter provides a foundation for future Internet research projects. Completing these activities will help your children increase comprehension skills, expand their understanding of the Internet, and develop multimedia capabilities. You may need to shape the type of research and level of processing for younger children to meet their needs. Feel free to modify the activities, such as removing a step, to meet the needs of your child. Monitor your child's expression to see if he is showing signs of frustration because the activity is too difficult or signs of boredom because the activity is too easy then modify the activity to help him succeed on his individual level. You could even make up your own activities. The following ideas might help.

- Choose and focus on a primary theme to excite younger children and motivate them to learn. Appropriate topics such as farm animals, seasons, the rainforest, planets, dinosaurs, or children around the world are proven interests of most children.

- Carefully choose a search engine that is suitable for younger children (without many advertisements or other distractions). Have children complete the research with you.

- After his research, have your child share the things he saw and learned on the website. Based on the information shared with you, draw a simple picture and write a sentence describing the picture. For example, if your child tells you about the moon, draw a picture of the moon and then write a sentence retelling the facts he has shared about the moon. After seeing you draw a picture and write a sentence, your child should be better prepared to complete the writing assignments such as Research Worksheet I (CD Supplement 6H) or Slide Worksheet (CD Supplement 6J).

- Have your child navigate the site using the mouse while you read the information to him. Then instruct your child to navigate the website and view the pictures. It would be best to locate a website with audio if your child is still learning to read.

- Review the steps of each activity several times and have your child repeat them to ensure comprehension. If the steps are repeated several times, your child will be able to visualize the process. Create a song to a familiar tune to teach the steps to creating a slide. When creating a slide, have younger children insert their name and pictures only.

- Before the younger children begin, have them circle the facts on the worksheet that they want to use in their slide. This will help them stay focused when typing.

## Internet Safety

In this chapter, some activities require Internet access. Remind your child to think about Internet safety during these activities. You may want to review the Internet safety tips on pages 10–11.

# Fun Decorations

An inspiring room atmosphere and decorated walls will excite your children and focus their attention on Internet research. Decorations can generate enthusiasm as well as provide another opportunity to teach research skills. Be creative in assembling decorations to motivate your children to learn about online research. The following are some ideas that might help you with decorations.

- Dedicate a section of your house to learning about Internet research. Refer to the information located in that area of your home throughout this chapter. Use a banner or letter cutouts to spell out "Internet Research," the topic of this chapter. Hang your child's completed work in this area.

- Hang up posters focusing on research or the Internet.

- Bring in a caged bird to keep in your house during this chapter or take a special nature walk to go bird watching. Allow your children to look at the birds and discuss the bird behaviors they see. Visit a website, such as www.audubon.org *or* www.birdwatching.com, to view different types of birds.

- Set up a fish aquarium and have your child research one of the fish that you have in the aquarium. You could also go online and create a virtual aquarium at websites such as www.virtualfishtank.com *or* www.facinity.com.

# Vocabulary

Review the following terms with your child so that he or she can have a basic understanding of the vocabulary used in this chapter. You could also have your child write the definitions in the Internet Research Vocabulary worksheet (CD Supplement 6M).

> **search engine:** A website designed to search the Internet for a particular topic.

> **website:** A location on the World Wide Web maintained by a group, company, or individual that includes a home page and various links containing information.

# NETS•S Addressed

1. **Creativity and Innovation**

   Students demonstrate creative thinking, construct knowledge, and develop innovative products and processes using technology. Students:

   a. apply existing knowledge to generate new ideas, products, or processes

   b. create original works as a means of personal or group expression

   c. use models and simulations to explore complex systems and issues

   d. identify trends and forecast possibilities

3. **Research and Information Fluency**

   Students apply digital tools to gather, evaluate, and use information. Students:

   a. plan strategies to guide inquiry

   b. locate, organize, analyze, evaluate, synthesize, and ethically use information from a variety of sources and media

   c. evaluate and select information sources and digital tools based on the appropriateness to specific tasks

   d. process data and report results

# Grades

There are many ways to determine your child's comprehension of researching using the Internet. Probably the best way is to observe your child as she searches for information online; therefore, during the activities, evaluate your child while she works. When deciding on the type of assessment, consider her age and abilities. The following are some suggestions that might help you to assess your child.

- Use the answer keys in the various activities to grade the supplements that your child completed. Base the grades on accuracy or completion. The answer keys can be found on the CD.

- You may want to use the Grade Book located in Appendix A at the back of this book to record your child's assignments and grades.

Keep a running record of your child's progress to determine comprehension and understanding of the content. Record these observations on paper or in the Grade Book.

- Ask your child to write down the definitions to the vocabulary words in this chapter using the Internet Research Vocabulary worksheet (CD Supplement 6M).

- Observe your child to determine her level of participation during instruction and individual Internet research. Check the completed slide from Activity 9 and make sure that your child used the appropriate information that you required.

- Print the slide and base the grade on successful insertion of the information required for her particular grade level or ability.

# Enrichment

Children are innately inquisitive, and this curiosity may prompt them to research new ideas once they have experienced independent research. Their access to worlds of information on the Internet with the freedom to explore it will inspire them to generate ideas and think of innovative concepts. Encourage your children to use the Internet not only to search for answers, but to help them think about ideas as well. Think of ways to inspire your child to use the Internet research skills as well as the multimedia technology skills learned during this chapter. A variety of challenging and motivating ideas are offered in the following list.

- Suggest that your child use other types of media for research, such as encyclopedias on CD or educational software.

- Your child could use Google Earth or another map navigation application to locate the habitat or migration patterns around the world of the bird or ocean animal he is researching.

- Have your child do an Internet research project on a natural disaster that occurred recently.

- Allow your child to go outside or look out the window to observe the weather.

- Have your child use HyperStudio, Kid Pix, or a different multimedia slide show application to create slides.

- Encourage your child to explore other aspects of the presentation application, such as slide transitions, music, and animation, when his slide is complete. This could generate a variety of fun extended activities using different multimedia elements.

- Your child could locate and insert the sound of his particular bird or ocean animal to be played when his slide show is played.

- Encourage your child to create his own slide on a fun topic such as family, dogs, the beach, or anything else that interests him.

- Go on a field trip to the zoo, a local bird sanctuary, or an aquarium to view and study the animals that your child researched during this chapter.

- Teach your child to use Boolean characters when searching using a search engine. Find out more about Boolean characters using these websites: http://adam.ac.uk/info/boolean.html *or* www.csa.com/help/Search_Tools/boolean_operators.html.

## Closure

Closure is an important part of the chapter because it allows your child to process the information learned. Your child should feel proud of her work when she has put forth her best effort. Give encouragement and compliments to your child on a job well done. Provide your child with a few moments to reflect on all she has accomplished and learned. The following are some suggestions for closure activities.

- Have your child share various research techniques or hints for quickly navigating the websites.

- Ask your child to share one fact she has learned while researching online. Ask your child to explain ways that the research concepts in this chapter could be useful when completing a research project in the future.

- Ask your child to share one thing she has learned about creating a slide.

Activity **1**

# Search Engines

## Goal

Your child will view various search engines and pick his favorite.

## Materials

- A computer with Internet access
- paper and pencil.

## Steps

### 1. Definition

Explain this definition of a search engine to your child: a search engine is a website designed to search the Internet for a particular topic. Have your child write down this definition.

### 2. Search Engines

Explain to your child that there are many different search engines. You could write them on a piece of paper for your child to look at during this activity.

- www.altavista.com
- www.askjeeves.com
- www.bing.com
- www.dogpile.com
- www.excite.com
- www.google.com
- www.hotbot.com
- www.metacrawler.com
- www.yahoo.com

### 3. View

Allow your child to view the various search engines online by typing their URLs into the address bar.

### 4. Favorite

Have your child select a favorite search engine and describe or write down what he likes about it.

**Tip**
Show your child how to make his favorite search engine his home page.

Activity **2**

# Bird Research

## Goal

Your child will use a search engine to gather facts on a particular bird and complete a worksheet.

## Materials

- Bird Worksheet (CD Supplement 6A)
- computer with Internet access
- pencil

## Steps

### 1. Topic

Allow your child to choose a particular bird to research, or you could assign a bird such as a robin, eagle, peacock, toucan, or albatross.

### 2. Type

Show your child how to type words into the search engine's search box and click Search or press Enter. Remind your child to type very specific words in the search box and type exactly what she needs to research. Some examples might include "owl habitat," "peacock diet," "albatross life cycle," or "eagle migration." If your child does not get the results or information she wants, have her type in different words or try a different search engine.

### 3. Open

Have your child open several webpages at once by right-clicking on the link, then selecting "open in a new tab or window." This will keep the main search engine open and allow her to look at many webpages in different windows.

## 4. Read

Talk to your child about how to read each webpage and decide whether it has the information needed. If not, close the window. You may want to teach your child about how to determine whether the website is a trustworthy source of information by viewing the web address, looking at the contact information, checking links, viewing the date that it was last updated, and checking for grammatical errors.

## 5. Worksheet

Have your child fill out the Bird Worksheet (CD Supplement 6A) using the information found online.

**Tips**

On a separate sheet of paper, have your child write down the words used in the search to help her remember which words produce the desired results. Also, have her write down the website used to gather the information, because it will be used on the Bird Worksheet (CD Supplement 6A).

While your child is typing and searching for information using a search engine, remind her to let you know if an inappropriate page pops up so you can close it immediately.

Activity 3

# Ocean Animal Research

## Goal

Your child will use a search engine to gather facts about a specific ocean animal and complete a worksheet.

## Materials

- Ocean Animal Worksheet (CD Supplement 6B)
- computer with Internet access
- pencil

## Steps

### 1. Topic

Allow your child to choose a particular ocean animal, or you could assign an ocean animal such as a hermit crab, an ocean sunfish, a sea otter, a dolphin, or a gray whale.

### 2. Type

Show your child how to type words into the search engine's search box and click Search or press Enter. Remind your child to type very specific words in the search box and type exactly what he needs to research. If your child does not get the results or information needed, help him think about different words to type or try a different search engine.

### 3. Open

Teach your child how to open several webpages at once by right-clicking on the link, then selecting "open in a new tab or window." This will keep the main search engine open and allow your child to look at many webpages in different windows.

## 4. Read

Talk to your child about how to read each webpage and decide whether it has the information needed. If not, close the window.

## 5. Worksheet

Your child will use the information from his search to fill out the Ocean Animal Worksheet (CD Supplement 6B).

**Tip**
On a separate sheet of paper, your child could write down the words used in his search and the website address that he used to get his facts.

Activity 4

# Natural Hazard Cards

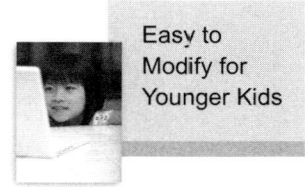

Easy to
Modify for
Younger Kids

## Goal

Your child will find the picture of a natural hazard on a website, after you hold up a card that shows a natural hazard.

## Materials

- Natural Hazard Cards (CD Supplement 6C)
- scissors
- computer with Internet access

## Steps

### 1. Prepare

Listed below are several websites for children on natural hazards. Become familiar with the websites ahead of time so that you can decide which sites will best meet the abilities of your child.

> **FEMA for Kids:** The Disaster Area:
> www.fema.gov/kids/dizarea.htm

> **Miami Museum of Science: Hurricane:**
> www.miamisci.org/hurricane/hurricane0.html

> **National Weather Service: Playtime for Kids:**
> www.nws.noaa.gov/om/reachout/kidspage.shtml

Print the Natural Hazard Cards (CD Supplement 6C) and cut them out. Glue them to construction paper for added durability.

### 2. Cards

Show the natural hazards cards to your child one at a time and read each card.

### 3. Website

Hold up one card and have your child search for a picture of that natural hazard using one of the websites.

### 4. Continue

Continue to hold up each card and have your child locate pictures and facts about the natural hazards. As your child is locating the pictures, you could read some of the interesting facts on the hazards aloud to your child, or have your child read the information to you.

**Tips**

You may want to talk to your child about how websites such as FEMA for Kids can help a family prepare for a natural disaster.

Display a natural hazard on the monitor from a website, and then your child must point to the matching card.

Your child could use the websites listed in this lesson to learn about other natural hazards.

Activity 5

# Natural Hazards Research

## Goal

Your child will use a website to complete a worksheet on natural hazards.

## Materials

- Natural Hazards Worksheet I or II (CD Supplement 6D or 6E)
- computer with Internet access
- pencil

## Steps

### 1. Prepare

Listed below are several websites that could be used to find information on natural hazards. Choose the one that will be the best for your child's age and abilities. Become familiar with the website ahead of time, so you will know how to navigate the site. Your child could use more than one website to complete the worksheets.

**FEMA for Kids: The Disaster Area:** www.fema.gov/kids/dizarea.htm

**Miami Museum of Science: Hurricane:**
www.miamisci.org/hurricane/hurricane0.html

**NASA: Natural Hazards Research Web Links:**
http://gcmd.gsfc.nasa.gov/Resources/pointers/hazards.html

**National Weather Service: National Hurricane Center:**
www.nhc.noaa.gov

**National Weather Service: Playtime for Kids:**
www.nws.noaa.gov/om/reachout/kidspage.shtml

**USGS TerraWeb for Kids: Links to Other Cool Websites:**
http://terraweb.wr.usgs.gov/TRS/kids/links.html

## 2. *Surf*

Show your child how to surf the website by clicking on different links to find the information needed to complete the worksheets. Allow your child to try navigating the site with your assistance.

## 3. *Worksheet*

Based on your child's skill level choose either Natural Hazards Worksheet I or II. Print the appropriate worksheet (CD Supplement 6D or 6E). Explain the instructions, answer any questions, and allow your child time to complete the worksheet.

## 4. *Check*

Use the information found on the website to check your child's worksheet.

Activity **6**

# Weather Bear

Easy to Modify for Younger Kids

## Goal

Your child will use the Internet to locate the weather for four different cities and record this information on a worksheet.

## Materials

- Weather Bear Worksheet (CD Supplement 6F)
- computer with Internet access
- crayons
- pencil

## Steps

### 1. Prepare

Choose a weather website, such as CNN.com's Weather (www.cnn.com/weather/) or Weather.com (www.weather.com), for your child to use to find out about the weather in different cities. Choose the one that will be the best for your child's age and abilities. Become familiar with the website ahead of time, so you will know how to navigate the site. Your child could use more than one website to complete the worksheet.

### 2. Weather

Ask your child to pick four cities to research. She will probably want to include the city or town where you currently live. Encourage your child to include cities that have different temperatures or weather so she can see the comparison and dress the bear differently on the worksheet. It may be fun to include cities of friends and family members who live in different places.

Have your child use the website to locate the weather for each city and record that information on the Weather Bear Worksheet (CD Supplement 6F). Have your child use crayons to color various clothes on the bear, such as a hat, a coat, boots, and a scarf, based on the different types of weather.

## 3. Check

Go over the worksheet with your child to ensure that she has completed the worksheet accurately.

**Tips**
Use a teddy bear and different types of clothes to have your child dress the bear according to the weather in different cities. Your child could also draw in clouds, sun, rain, or snow to represent the weather in the weather bear box.

Activity 7

# Weather Chart

## Goal

Your child will fill in a weather chart for five days by viewing the weather online.

## Materials

- Weather Chart (CD Supplement 6G)
- computer with Internet access
- pencil

## Steps

### 1. Prepare

Choose a weather website such as CNN.com's Weather (www.cnn.com/weather/) or Weather.com (www.weather.com) for your child to use to find out about the weather in different cities. Choose the one that will be the best for your child's age and abilities. Become familiar with the website ahead of time, so you will know how to navigate the site. Your child could use more than one website to complete the weather chart.

### 2. Chart

Have your child choose five cities to research. Encourage your child to include cities that have different temperatures or weather so he can see the comparison. Your child will probably want to include your current city or town. It may be fun to include cities of friends and family members who live in different places.

Have your child use the weather site to locate the information (weather, temperature, wind, and humidity) for each city for five days and record it on the Weather Chart (CD Supplement 6G).

## 3. Check

When your child has finished the weather chart, go over any noticeable weather patterns and anything your child learned about viewing the weather online.

> **Tip**
> Have your child record the weather for each city for a month, and then make charts displaying the various temperatures in the different cities.

Activity **8**

# *Choose a Topic*

## Goal

Your child will use a search engine to conduct research on a topic of her choice and complete a worksheet.

## Materials

- Research Worksheet I or II (CD Supplement 6H or 6I)
- computer with Internet access
- pencil

## Steps

### *1. Topic*

Have your child choose a topic that she would like to research on her own. It could be a current science or social studies topic that she is learning about, or just something that interests her.

### *2. Worksheet*

Your child will research her topic using a search engine and then complete Research Worksheet I or II (CD Supplement 6H or 6I).

### *3. Review*

Give your child enough time to complete the worksheet, then go over the information she recorded.

**Tip**
Have your child write down the websites used to locate her information because she may need to refer back to the sites for pictures or more information when creating the slide in Activity 9.

Activity 9

# Create a Slide

Easy to
Modify for
Younger Kids

## Goal

Your child will fill in blanks on a worksheet and then create a slide.

## Materials

- Slide Worksheet (CD Supplement 6J)
- Sample Slides (CD Supplement 6K)
- pencil
- computer with multimedia presentation software such as Microsoft PowerPoint or OpenOffice Impress Presentation

## Steps

### 1. Prepare

Use the websites below to learn how to create a multimedia slide show with your child. The specific instructions for designing a slide show depend on the type of presentation software being used on your computer. The following websites may be used for tutorials, online help, and downloads. OpenOffice Impress Presentation can be downloaded from the OpenOffice.org website (www.openoffice.org).

**Microsoft PowerPoint**

**ActDen PowerPoint in the Classroom:** www.actden.com/pp/

**Education World PowerPoint Tutorial:**
www.educationworld.com/a_tech/tutorials/ew_ppt.htm

**Internet For Classrooms Microsoft PowerPoint:**
www.internet4classrooms.com/on-line_powerpoint.htm

**PowerPoint Tutorial:**
http://oregonstate.edu/instruction/ed596/ppoint/pphome.htm

Also, PowerPoint offers searches in the Help menu. Search for specific topics if you need help with this program.

### OpenOffice Impress Presentation

**About.com OpenOffice Impress:** http://presentationsoft.about.com/od/
openofficeimpress/tp/071021openoffice_beginguide.htm  *–and–*
http://presentationsoft.about.com/od/openofficeimpress/Open_Office_
Impress_Free_Presentation_Software.htm

**LearnOpenOffice.org:** www.learnopenoffice.org/contents.htm

**OpenOffice.org Impress Tutorial:** http://documentation.openoffice.org/
tutorials/cospa/Cospa_Impress_Tutorial.pdf

**Tutorials for OpenOffice:**
www.tutorialsforopenoffice.org/category_index/presentation.html

**OpenOffice.org Impress In Pictures:** http://inpics.net/impress.html

Also, OpenOffice Impress offers searches in the Help menu. Search for
specific topics if you need help with this program.

## 2. Write

Have your child write down the information to be included on his
slide on the Slide Worksheet (CD Supplement 6J). Your child can select
one of the topics already researched in this chapter to complete this
worksheet.

## 3. Create

Open the multimedia presentation software that your child will use
to create a slide. Show your child how to create a new slide, insert
text, insert graphics, and create animation. Show your child how to
save the slide. Then allow your child to use the information from
his slide worksheet to create his slide. Your child's personality and
unique talents will be expressed as he creates his slide. You may want
to share the Sample Slides (CD Supplement 6K) so your child can see a
completed slide.

**Tips**
Show your child how to change background, font, and colors.
Allow your child to make a fun slide with his name and any
pictures he wants to include. In Chapter 9, your child will create
a multimedia slide show that includes several slides.

Activity **10**

# Slide Presentation

Easy to Modify for Younger Kids

## Goal

Your child will present her slide.

## Materials

- Presentation Grading Sheet (CD Supplement 6L)
- saved multimedia slide from Activity 9
- computer with multimedia presentation software

## Steps

### 1. Prepare

Open the slide using the multimedia presentation software on your computer.

### 2. Practice

Show your child how to display the slide in presentation mode. Talk to your child about all that you expect during the presentation. Allow your child to practice the presentation on her own.

### 3. Presentation

Allow your child to present her slide to a friend or another family member. Use the Presentation Grading Sheet (CD Supplement 6L) to assess your child during the presentation.

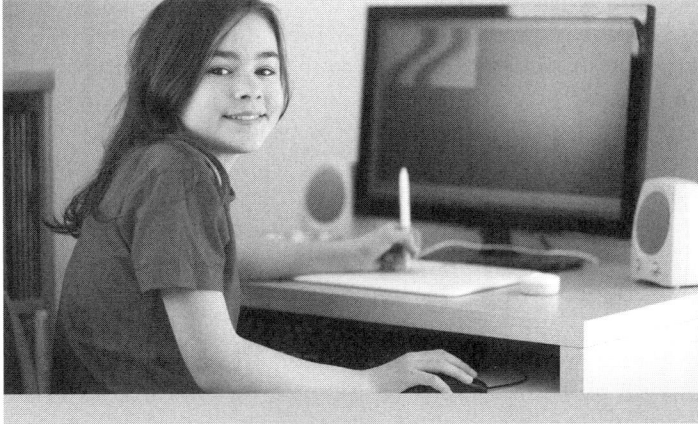

## Chapter 7

# Peripheral Devices

## Objective

Children will research, identify, and describe 25 peripheral devices using a slide show, a scavenger hunt, books, games, research, and learning cards.

## Purpose

Convey to your children the significance of knowing about peripheral devices. Your children will work harder to learn these terms if they know it will help them in the future. Explain that it is important to know the names and functions of basic peripheral devices to successfully operate computers. Think of a unique way to provide reasons for learning so your children will be able to personally apply this information to their lives.

# Activities Overview

This foundational chapter will help your child understand basic peripheral devices and their meanings through a variety of activities. This chapter will provide your child with the foundation and terminology to discuss and understand the rudiments of computers. Carefully consider which activities will benefit your child depending on his or her age, abilities, and learning style. The following chart categorizes each activity to help you to plan the lessons. Some children may be able to complete all of the activities, whereas others would benefit by focusing more time on a few key activities. Certain children may require a more structured environment, whereas a self-motivated child could be given more freedom.

Children will have several opportunities to identify and examine the devices. At the completion of this chapter, your child should have a sound understanding of basic technology concepts. Encourage your children as they work; they will be able to do a lot more if they feel that you believe in them.

| Activities | Worksheet | Modifiable* | Internet Access | Game | Learning Cards | Slide Show | Arts and Crafts | Answer Key |
|---|---|---|---|---|---|---|---|---|
| 1. Peripheral Devices Slide Show | | ✔ | | | | ✔ | | |
| 2. Internet Research | ✔ | | ✔ | | | | | ✔ |
| 3. Identify the Devices | | ✔ | | ✔ | | | | |
| 4. Make a Book | | ✔ | | | | | ✔ | |
| 5. Website Scavenger Hunt | | | ✔ | ✔ | | | | |
| 6. Coloring Book | ✔ | ✔ | | | | | ✔ | |
| 7. Peripheral Device Cards | ✔ | | | | ✔ | | | |
| 8. Input: Output: Storage | ✔ | | | | ✔ | | | |
| 9. Matching Game | | | | ✔ | | ✔ | | |
| 10. Quiz | ✔ | | | | | | | ✔ |

* Easily modifiable for younger children

Remember, don't hurry to complete an activity just to have it completed; your child should work at his or her own pace and really understand the concepts. Create a positive atmosphere while encouraging your child to learn with confidence. To get started, you may decide to plan a fun activity to inspire your child and focus your child's attention on technology. A lively event will prompt children to focus on the peripheral devices, and they will be more interested and ready to learn.

## CD Supplements

The following chart lists all of the CD supplements for this chapter and provides the CD filename, supplement title, and activity number. To make locating and using these supplements faster and easier, it is recommended that you copy all files to your hard drive before beginning the lessons.

| CD Filename | Title | Activity |
|---|---|---|
| 7A | Peripheral Devices Slide Show | 1, 9 |
| 7B | Peripheral Devices Worksheet I | 2 |
| 7C | Peripheral Devices Worksheet II | 2 |
| 7D | Peripheral Devices Worksheet I Answers | 2 |
| 7E | Peripheral Devices Worksheet II Answers | 2 |
| 7F | Peripheral Devices Coloring book | 6 |
| 7G | Peripheral Device Cards | 7, 8 |
| 7H | Peripheral Devices Quiz I | 10 |
| 7I | Peripheral Devices Quiz II | 10 |
| 7J | Peripheral Devices Quiz III | 10 |
| 7K | Peripheral Devices Quiz I Answers | 10 |
| 7L | Peripheral Devices Quiz II Answers | 10 |
| 7M | Peripheral Devices Quiz III Answers | 10 |
| 7N | Peripheral Devices Vocabulary | Optional |

## Variations for Younger Children

Younger children learn differently and are motivated to explore concepts by different factors. Provide younger children with several opportunities to learn the peripheral devices, taking into account their various learning styles. Feel free to modify the activities, such as removing a step, to meet the needs of your child. Monitor your child's expression to see if he is showing signs of frustration because the activity is too difficult or signs of boredom because the activity is too easy then modify the activity to help him succeed on his individual level. You could even make up your own activities. The following ideas may help.

- Concentrate on fewer peripheral devices throughout the chapter.
- Use one website consistently when viewing the peripheral devices online.
- Have younger children participate in more hands-on experiences by encouraging them to examine the peripheral devices.
- Use a puppet to explain various devices.
- Make up a song to a popular nursery tune, incorporating the various devices. Sing this song with your child while pointing to the devices to aid in learning.

## Internet Safety

In this chapter, some activities require Internet access. Remind your child to think about Internet safety during these activities. You may want to review the Internet safety tips on pages 10–11.

## Fun Decorations

An inspiring room atmosphere and decorated walls will excite your children and focus their attention on technology. Decorations can generate enthusiasm as well as provide another opportunity to teach your children about peripheral devices. Be inventive as you plan the room decorations, and remember to have fun! The following are some ideas that might help you with decorations.

- Print each page of the Peripheral Devices Slide Show (CD Supplement 7A), glue the words and pictures to construction paper, and then hang them on a wall or door. It would work nicely to print six slides per page so you will be ready for Activity 9: Matching Game.

- Print the Peripheral Device Cards (CD Supplement 7G), glue them to large stars, and hang them from the ceiling. Make the stars by cutting out star shapes from yellow or white construction paper. You will also be able to use these cards for Activity 7: Peripheral Device Cards and Activity 8: Input: Output: Storage.

- Dedicate a section of your house to learning the peripheral devices. Refer to the information located in that area of your home throughout this chapter. Use a banner or letter cutouts to spell out "Peripheral Devices," the topic of this chapter. Hang completed Peripheral Devices work in this area.

- Change the screensaver or the desktop background of your computer to a picture of a peripheral device that your child will be learning about in this chapter.

## Vocabulary

The vocabulary terms in this chapter are organized according to storage, input, and output devices to help your child better understand peripheral devices. Some devices could be considered to be in more than one category. However, for the purpose of instruction, they have been placed in the category that most closely represents the meaning and purpose of the device.

Review the following terms with your child so that he or she can have a basic understanding of the vocabulary used in this chapter. You could also have your child write the definitions in the Peripheral Devices Vocabulary worksheet (CD Supplement 7N).

> **input device:** A device used to enter information into a computer.
>
> **output device:** A device that receives data from a computer.
>
> **peripheral device:** A piece of computer hardware that is connected to a computer.
>
> **storage device:** A device that reads and writes digital media such as optical discs, USB drives, or tape.

## Storage Device Examples

**CD drive:** The component that reads and writes information to CDs (compact discs).

**DVD drive:** The component that reads and writes information to the DVDs (digital video discs).

**floppy drive:** The component that reads and writes information to floppy disks.

**hard drive:** A device that reads and writes information very quickly. Most hard drives are built into the computer and store critical information such as your operating system and most applications such as Microsoft Office as well as data.

**tape drive:** The component that reads and writes information to magnetic tape (similar to a tape recorder).

**USB drive:** A small storage device that plugs into a computer's USB (Universal Serial Bus) port.

## Input Device Examples

**barcode reader:** A device that reads barcodes.

**data glove:** A glove that fits over a hand of a person and records movements to a computer.

**digital camera:** A camera that records pictures in a digital format.

**fingerprint scanner:** A scanner used to identify a fingerprint for security.

**joystick:** A device with a vertical lever that can be tilted in various ways, most often used to play video games.

**keyboard:** A hardware device consisting of buttons (keys) that the user presses to type characters into a computer.

**microphone:** A device that converts sound waves into electrical impulses that can be stored digitally.

**mouse:** A hand-operated data input device that moves the cursor on a computer screen.

**scanner:** A device used to scan and translate images into a digital format to be read by the computer.

**trackball:** A device with a moveable ball that is operated by the hand to control the cursor.

**webcam:** A video camera that is connected to the Internet.

## Output Device Examples

**computer projector:** A device that projects images from a computer onto a screen.

**headphones:** Small speakers mounted over the ears that convert electrical signals into sounds.

**interactive whiteboard:** A large interactive board used with a computer and a projector.

**monitor:** A video screen that takes signals from a computer and displays the information.

**portable media player:** A handheld device that can play audio and/or video files.

**printer:** A device that prints text or graphics on paper.

**smart phone:** A handheld communication device with computing capabilities..

**speakers:** Electronic equipment used to play sound.

# NETS•S Addressed

6.  **Technology Operations and Concepts**

    Students demonstrate a sound understanding of technology concepts, systems, and operations. Students:

    a.  understand and use technology systems

    b.  select and use applications effectively and productively

    c.  troubleshoot systems and applications

    d.  transfer current knowledge to the learning of new technologies

# Grades

Think of the best way to determine your child's comprehension of the peripheral devices for each activity. This is your child's opportunity to demonstrate his individual understanding of the peripheral devices and their functions. Throughout each activity, evaluate your child while he works. When deciding on the type of assessment, consider his age and abilities. The following are some suggestions that might help you to assess your child.

- Use the answer keys in the various activities to grade the supplements that your child completed. Base the grades on accuracy or completion. The answer keys can be found on the CD.

- Keep a running record of your child's progress to determine comprehension and understanding of the content. Record these observations on paper or in the Grade Book (Appendix A). Ask your child to write down the definitions to the vocabulary words using the Peripheral Devices Vocabulary worksheet (CD Supplement 7N). Observe your child as he researches the peripheral devices on the Internet, and document his efforts.

# Enrichment

Learning takes place all of the time, so motivate your child to learn more about peripheral devices on her own. The excitement of learning about peripheral devices will probably motivate your child to learn more about technology. Children could become actively involved by deciding for themselves which enrichment activity to complete. You could plan additional ways to expand your children's minds and their comprehension of computers. Be creative in thinking of an advanced assignment for high achievers. A variety of challenging and motivating ideas are offered in the following list.

- Ask your child to create and design a futuristic peripheral device that will help society. Have your child draw a diagram and write a paragraph describing the purpose of this peripheral device. Instruct your child to explain the individual components of the device and how it will work.

- Take a field trip to a computer parts store (or any store with computers) and write down all of the peripheral devices that your child finds. Discuss why these devices are peripheral devices and discuss the purpose of the device. When you get home, your child could research these devices on the Internet.

- To stimulate higher-level thinking, require your child to locate and describe on paper the similarities in two similar peripheral devices, such as speakers and headphones, joystick and mouse, or CD drive and DVD drive.

- Encourage your child to research more input and output peripheral devices not included in this chapter, such as a memory card reader, eye tracking device, Internet phone, Bluetooth headset, or modem. Ask her to illustrate and write a sentence describing the device.

- Take a few pictures of your child, print them, and hang them up on a wall. Talk to your child about the differences between film and digital photography. Take a picture of your child using a digital camera, load the pictures onto your computer, and allow her to open her picture and copy it to a blank document. She could then type a few sentences describing herself and print it out.

- Have your child draw a picture of an entire computer system, utilizing at least 10 of the peripheral devices discussed in the chapter. Then ask your child to write a paragraph explaining how the devices work.

- Ask your child to research and create a poster explaining the differences in the media associated with the storage devices discussed in this chapter, such as CD-ROM (Compact Disc Read-Only Memory), CD-R (Compact Disc Recordable), CD-RW (Compact Disc Rewriteable), DVD (Digital Video Disc), and DVD-R (Digital Video Disc Recordable).

- Encourage a discussion on the different aspects and interesting facts regarding the peripheral devices, including:
  - Various drives in a computer (CD, DVD, floppy, tape, hard disk)
  - Types of compact discs (CD-ROM, CD-R, CD-RW)
  - Different styles of printers (inkjet, laser, thermal, wax; color or black and white)

## Closure

The closing of each chapter is an important part of the learning process because children are given a few minutes to reflect on all they have learned and make the information their own.

The following are some suggestions for closure activities.

- Have your child share navigation techniques that did and did not work when researching online. This could help children with future Internet research. Require your child to be accountable for knowing the peripheral devices and their functions.

- Ask, "What have you learned concerning peripheral devices?" Encourage your child to share a few interesting facts or trivia that he has learned about peripheral devices. Have your child talk about an interesting peripheral device used at home and describe the way the device helps the family.

- Encourage your child to share the concepts learned and ways these concepts will assist him in the future.

Activity 1

# Peripheral Devices Slide Show

Easy to Modify for Younger Kids

## Goal

Your child will recite the 25 peripheral devices using a slide show presentation.

## Materials

- Peripheral Devices Slide Show (CD Supplement 7A)
- computer

## Steps

### 1. Prepare

Open the Peripheral Devices Slide Show (CD Supplement 7A). Click Slide Show > View Slide Show when you are ready to begin.

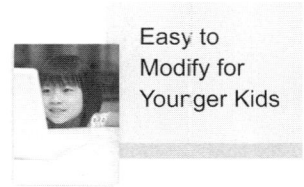

### 2. Assess

The slide show displays a picture of the peripheral device then the name of the peripheral device. As you advance each slide, have your child name any of the peripheral devices that he already knows. You may be surprised at the peripheral devices your child already knows! This is a great way to assess the information your child previously had about the peripheral devices in this chapter.

### 3. Recite

Play the slide show again and have your child recite the peripheral devices as they appear on the screen. Tell your child to repeat after you if he needs help saying the name of the device. Replay the slide show a few times (if needed) to teach your child to correctly recite the names of all these parts.

**Tips**

During the presentation, discuss the difference between output, input, and storage devices. Definitions are listed at the beginning of this chapter in the Vocabulary section.

Add something new and interesting to the presentation such as music, animation, or various slide backgrounds.

To stimulate higher-level thinking skills, during Step 2: Assess, have your child to write down the name of the device and the function of the device for any term that he already knows. Ask him to include whether the device is an input, output, or storage device.

Activity **2**

# Internet Research

## Goal

Your child will research peripheral devices on a website, and then draw illustrations of the devices and write the purpose of the devices on a worksheet.

## Materials

- Peripheral Devices Worksheet I or II (CD Supplement 7B or 7C)
- Peripheral Devices Worksheet I or II Answers (CD Supplement 7D or 7E)
- pencil
- computer with Internet access

## Steps

### 1. Prepare

Listed below are several websites that could be used to find the peripheral devices. Become familiar with the websites ahead of time so that you can decide which sites will best meet the abilities of your child.

**How Stuff Works:** www.howstuffworks.com/pc.htm  –and–
    http://computer.howstuffworks.com/computer-peripherals-channel.htm
    **Note:** Use the How Stuff Works search engine.

**Introduction to Computers:**
    www.grassrootsdesign.com/intro/hardware.php

**Jan's Illustrated Computer Literacy 101:**
    www.jegsworks.com/Lessons/lesson3/lesson3-1.htm

**Kids Domain Computer Connections: Computers Inside & Out:**
    www.kidsdomain.com/brain/computer/lesson/comp_les1.html

**TekMom's Technology Buzzwords for Students:**
    www.tekmom.com/buzzwords/#SearchBox

## 2. *Teach*

Show your child how to navigate the website and ways to locate the pictures and purposes of the peripheral devices. You may want to locate one of the devices together with your child.

## 3. *Worksheets*

Choose either the Peripheral Devices Worksheet I or II (CD Supplement 7B or 7C), depending on the abilities of your child.

If using Peripheral Devices Worksheet I (CD Supplement 7B), have your child locate the peripheral device on a website, and then draw an illustration of the device in the box provided.

You may need to help your child locate the peripheral devices. It may be fun to read some of the information on the sites while discussing the devices together. Strive to focus on the devices that seem to interest your child.

If using Peripheral Devices Worksheet II (CD Supplement 7C), have your child locate the peripheral device on a website, then draw an illustration and write the purpose of the device in the boxes provided.

Your child should incorporate critical thinking skills when determining the purpose of each device and writing the purpose using her own words. Your child should be excited to begin this Internet activity. Provide encouragement and support to help her discover information on her own.

## 4. *Check*

Use the Peripheral Device Worksheet I or II Answers (CD Supplements 7D and 7E) to check her work. Your child could also use the answer key to self-check her work.

Activity 3

# Identify the Devices

Easy to
Modify for
Younger Kids

## Goal

Your child will locate and identify peripheral devices.

## Materials

- 25 peripheral devices (use as many as you have):

    **Storage Devices:** CD drive, DVD drive, USB drive, floppy drive, hard drive, tape drive

    **Input Devices:** barcode reader, data glove, digital camera, fingerprint scanner, joystick, keyboard, microphone, mouse, scanner, trackball, webcam

    **Output Devices:** computer projector, headphones, interactive whiteboard, monitor, smart phone, portable media player, printer, speakers

## Steps

### 1. Prepare

Use as many actual devices as possible to give children the opportunity to see the physical device. You could use a picture to represent ones you don't have. Place the peripheral devices on a table or a specific location in a room.

### 2. Locate

Ask, "Can you find the speakers?" Commend your child after he locates the speakers. If he is unable to locate the speakers on the table, give a hint to help him in locating them. For example, say, "This is the device that plays sound."

## 3. Examine

Continue this game with the other devices. After locating the device, allow your child to look at it and examine it closely. Discuss any interesting details about the devices.

## 4. Repeat

Repeat this activity asking more specific questions, or even the purpose of the device such as, "Can you find the device that reads information from a compact disc?" If your child is unable to locate the CD drive on the table, give another hint to help him find the CD drive.

**Tips**

Take a field trip to a local computer store and look at the various peripheral devices with your child. Point out various peripheral devices in this chapter when you are at the grocery store, library, post office, or another store that uses these devices.

This is a great hands-on activity for children who learn best by seeing and touching. Much of technology is virtual; however, this activity involves viewing and touching the actual objects.

Activity **4**

# Make a Book

Easy to
Modify for
Younger Kids

## Goal

Your child will make a book on peripheral devices.

## Materials

- markers or colored pencils
- white paper (any size or style)
- stapler
- construction paper (optional)
- stickers (optional)

## Steps

### 1. Draw

Ask your child to draw an illustration of one of the peripheral devices on a piece of blank paper while looking at the actual device or a picture of the device.

### 2. Label

Have your child write the name of the device on the paper. Allow her to be creative and write it anywhere on the paper.

### 3. Purpose

Have your child write the purpose of the device, describing what it does. Repeat steps 1–3 for each device.

### 4. Decorate

Allow your child to decorate each page using markers, colored pencils, or stickers. Encourage your child to make a cover for the book from construction paper. Staple the pages together to make a book.

## 5. Read

Allow your child to read the book to you or someone else.

> **Tip**
> Encourage your child to cut out pictures of these devices from old magazines or catalogs and glue them to the specific page of that term in her book.

Activity **5**

# Website Scavenger Hunt

## Goal

Your child will search for certain peripheral device terms, pictures, or facts on websites.

## Materials

- computer with Internet access
- paper and pencil

## Steps

### 1. Prepare

Choose a website and make a list of certain devices, pictures, or facts that you would like your child to find on that site. Use some devices that your child needs to practice, or choose new peripheral devices that you would like to teach.

**How Stuff Works:** www.howstuffworks.com/pc.htm  *–and–*
    http://computer.howstuffworks.com/computer-peripherals-channel.htm
    **Note:** Use the How Stuff Works search engine.

**Introduction to Computers:**
    www.grassrootsdesign.com/intro/hardware.php

**Jan's Illustrated Computer Literacy 101:**
    www.jegsworks.com/Lessons/lesson3/lesson3-1.htm

**Kids Domain Computer Connections: Computers Inside & Out:**
    www.kidsdomain.com/brain/computer/lesson/comp_les1.html

**TekMom's Technology Buzzwords for Students:**
    www.tekmom.com/buzzwords/#SearchBox

## 2. Directions

Explain to your child that he should go to the website and look for a particular word, such as "camera," or a picture, such as a picture of a printer, or a certain fact, such as the purpose of a printer. Depending on the age of your child, you may need to help him navigate the site.

## 3. Begin

Have your child open the site and begin searching for the items on your list. You may want to ask him to make a check mark next to the item on your list when he locates it on the site.

**Tips**
Time your child for each item to find out which items were the quickest to locate and which ones were more difficult. Create a fill-in-the-blank worksheet for your child by writing a sentence from a website leaving one word out. Your child must search for the missing word.

Activity **6**

# Coloring Book

Easy to
Modify for
Younger Kids

## Goal

Your child will color pictures in a coloring book about peripheral devices.

## Materials

- Peripheral Devices Coloring Book (CD Supplement 7F), printed in black and white
- computer with Internet access
- crayons, markers, or colored pencils

## Steps

### 1. Websites

Choose a website from Activity 5 to show your child pictures and information about the peripheral devices.

### 2. Color

Allow your child to use crayons, markers, or colored pencils to color the devices on the Peripheral Devices Coloring Book (CD Supplement 7F) as you read about them on the website.

### 3. Discover

Your child may want to explore some of the other peripheral devices shown on the screen. Give her an opportunity to explore with your guidance.

**Tips**
For fun, your child could make her own book by stapling the pages of the coloring book together. She could make a cover for the book using construction paper.

Activity **7**

# *Peripheral Device Cards*

## Goal

Your child will identify peripheral devices by labeling them with the matching peripheral device cards.

## Materials

- Peripheral Device Cards (CD Supplement 7G)
- scissors
- tape
- peripheral devices (use as many as you have)

## Steps

### 1. Prepare

Print the Peripheral Device Cards (CD Supplement 7G) and then cut them out. Glue them to construction paper for added durability.

### 2. Discuss

As you show each card, give your child an opportunity to tell you about the device and explain the purpose of the device to you. If your child is still learning to read, just read the card for him, and then allow him to share. You could also describe the function of a particular device, and have your child find the corresponding card.

### 3. Label

Have your child label the peripheral devices in the room by taping the word cards to them. If you don't have some of the peripheral devices, just allow your child to explain what it looks like or what it does.

## 4. Check

Check each card to see if your child put the card in the correct place. If your child needs extra practice, do the activity again.

**Tips**
Try to have your child memorize the names of the various peripheral devices. If you show your enthusiasm and interest while teaching, your child will catch the excitement to learn. Think of a fun way to instruct your child and motivate him by actively involving him in the activity. Hold up one of the Peripheral Device Cards (CD Supplement 7G) and have your child write the purpose of the device on a piece of paper.

Activity **8**

# *Input: Output: Storage*

## Goal

Your child will determine if the peripheral device is an input, output, or storage device.

## Materials

- Peripheral Device Cards (from Activity 7, CD Supplement 7G)
- Three pieces of paper
- Marker

## Steps

### 1. Prepare

At the top of a piece of paper write "Input Devices," on another piece write "Output Devices," and on the last piece of paper write "Storage Devices."

### 2. Discuss

Discuss the differences among the three types of peripheral devices.

> **storage device:** A device that reads and writes digital media such as optical discs, USB drives, or tape.

> **input device:** A device used to enter information into a computer.

> **output device:** A device that receives data from a computer.

## 3. Cards

Have your child put the Peripheral Device Cards (CD Supplement 7G) on the paper with the corresponding type of device. For example, have your child place the printer card on the paper labeled "Output Devices" because a printer is an output device. Please note that some new devices could be categorized as a combination of input, output, and storage.

## 4. Check

Use the vocabulary section at the beginning of this chapter to determine if the device is a storage, input, or output device.

**Tip**
Have your child place the actual device on the piece of paper or in a certain place instead of using the cards.

Activity 9

# Matching Game

## Goal

Your child will match peripheral device picture cards with peripheral device name cards.

## Materials

- Peripheral Devices Slide Show (CD Supplement 7A)
- scissors
- printer
- paper for printer
- construction paper (optional)

## Steps

### 1. Prepare

Print the Peripheral Devices Slide Show (CD Supplement 7A), printing several slides per page, then cut the slides apart. It would work nicely to print six slides per page. You will not need the title pages or the input/output/storage slides. You may need to glue or tape the slides to construction paper so your child cannot see through the paper.

### 2. Review

Before you begin, you may want to review the picture of each device and the name of the device with your child.

### 3. Position Cards

Place all of the picture cards and name cards upside down on the floor or table to play the matching game. You could choose only a few of the cards and their matches so that your child can play a shorter version first.

## 4. Play

To play, have your child pick up one card and try to find the corresponding card. For example, to get a match, your child will need a card that says "camera" and the card with a picture of a camera. When your child gets a match, he keeps it. Your child should continue playing until he has matched all of the cards. Then, he can mix them all up and play again.

**Tip**
Play this game with your child, and another sibling or friend could play as well. When all of the matches have been paired, the person with the most matches at the end of the game wins.

Activity **10**

# *Quiz*

## Goal

Your child will take a peripheral devices quiz.

## Materials

- Peripheral Devices Quiz I, II, or III (CD Supplements 7H, 7I, or 7J)
- Peripheral Devices Quiz I, II, or III Answers (CD Supplements 7K, 7L, or 7M)
- computer or pencil

## Steps

### 1. Prepare

Decide which Peripheral Devices Quiz (I, II, or III) will best meet the needs of your child. Print the appropriate quiz (CD Supplement 7H, 7I, or 7J).

### 2. Quiz

Explain the instructions at the top of the assessment. Go over any questions. Give your child enough time to take the quiz to determine all that she has learned about peripheral devices during this chapter.

### 3. Check

Use the Peripheral Devices Quiz I, II, or III Answers (CD Supplements 7K, 7L, or 7M) to grade your child's work. Go over any missed questions with your child.

## Chapter 8

# Communicating Using the Internet

## Objective

Children will learn the basics of how to communicate using e-mail (electronic mail), IM (instant messaging), VoIP (Voice over Internet Protocol), and videoconferencing using slide shows, worksheets, and learning cards, as well as hands-on Internet communication experiences.

## Purpose

Show your children that this chapter has value for them so that they will be committed to learning. Talk about how popular Internet communication has become in recent years, replacing other forms of communication. Make this chapter meaningful by explaining the importance of knowing how to communicate using the Internet appropriately and ethically. Talk about ways that people use e-mail, IM, VoIP, and videoconferences in a work environment, such as a school office communicating with classroom teachers or nurses communicating with doctors at hospitals.

## Activities Overview

The activities in this chapter offer a solid foundation for communicating using e-mail, IM, VoIP, and videoconferencing. At the completion of this chapter, your child should have a sound understanding of communicating using e-mail, IM, VoIP, and videoconferences. The following chart categorizes each activity to help you to plan the lessons.

To get started, you may decide to plan a fun activity to inspire your child and focus your child's attention on Internet communication. You could write and send a special e-mail message with a subject labeled "secret message" to your child so that he or she can open it during the e-mail activity. A lively event will prompt children to focus on communicating using the Internet, and they will be more interested and ready to learn.

| Activities | Worksheet | Modifiable* | Internet Access | Game | Learning Cards | Slide Show | Arts and Crafts | Answer Key |
|---|---|---|---|---|---|---|---|---|
| 1. E-mail Slide Show | | ✔ | | | | ✔ | | |
| 2. How E-mail Works | ✔ | | | | | | | ✔ |
| 3. Send an E-mail | ✔ | | ✔ | | | | | |
| 4. Instant Messaging Slide Show | | ✔ | | | | ✔ | | |
| 5. Send an Instant Message (IM) | | | ✔ | | | | | |
| 6. Emoticons and Acronyms Slide Show | | ✔ | | | | ✔ | ✔ | |
| 7. Emoticons and Acronyms Quiz | ✔ | | | ✔ | | | | ✔ |
| 8. VoIP and Videoconferencing Slide Show | ✔ | ✔ | | | | ✔ | | |
| 9. VoIP Phone Call | | ✔ | ✔ | | | | | |
| 10. Videoconference | | ✔ | ✔ | | | | | |

* Easily modifiable for younger children

# CD Supplements

The following chart lists all of the CD supplements for this chapter and provides the CD filename, supplement title, and activity number. To make locating and using these supplements faster and easier, it is recommended that you copy all files to your hard drive before beginning the lessons.

| CD Filename | Title | Activity |
|---|---|---|
| 8A | E-mail Slide Show | 1 |
| 8B | E-mail Procedures Worksheet | 2 |
| 8C | E-mail Procedures Worksheet Answers | 2 |
| 8D | E-mail Message Worksheet | 3 |
| 8E | Instant Messaging Slide Show | 4 |
| 8F | Emoticons and Acronyms Slide Show | 6 |
| 8G | Emoticon and Acronym Cards | 7 |
| 8H | Emoticons Quiz | 7 |
| 8I | Emoticons and Acronyms Quiz | 7 |
| 8J | Emoticons Quiz Answers | 7 |
| 8K | Emoticons and Acronyms Quiz Answers | 7 |
| 8L | VoIP and Videoconferencing Slide Show | 8 |
| 8M | VoIP and Videoconferencing Worksheet | 8 |
| 8N | Communicating Using the Internet Vocabulary | Optional |

# Variations for Younger Children

Children are exposed to the computer at an early age and should learn how to communicate appropriately when using the Internet. Prepare appropriate activities that will allow your child to explore ideas while giving him sufficient exposure to the Internet communications concepts. Feel free to modify the activities, such as removing a step, to meet the needs of your child. Monitor your child's expression to see if he is showing signs of frustration because the activity is too difficult or signs of boredom because the activity is too easy; then modify the activity to help him succeed on his individual level. You could even make up your own activities. The following ideas may help.

- Create a booklet by printing some of the slides from the slide shows (CD Supplements 8A, 8E, 8F, and 8L) so that your children can read about the Internet communications concepts and look at the pictures on their own. Have them color this booklet for added fun! Also have them look at this booklet during the slide shows.

- Allow your child to send and receive simple IM messages. Here are a few suggestions of short, fun statements your child could type:

  - An emoticon

  - An acronym

  - His favorite color, song, or sport

  - An answer to a question such as: "What do you want to be when you grow up?'

  - His answer to this fill-in-the-blank statement: "I'm going to the moon in a spaceship and I want to take _____."

- Concentrate on a few of the Internet safety terms, instead of all of the terms that are discussed throughout the chapter. You may want to expose your child to all of the terms, but focus on one or two terms.

## Internet Safety

In this chapter, some activities require Internet access. Remind your child to think about Internet safety during these activities. You may want to review the Internet safety tips on pages 10–11.

## Fun Decorations

Do something different at your house for this chapter by creating an environment that will excite your child about Internet communications. Decorations can generate enthusiasm as well as provide another opportunity to teach your child about communicating using the Internet. Be inventive as you plan the room decorations, and remember to have fun! The following are some ideas that might help you with decorations.

- Print one or two pages from each slide show in this chapter, glue them to construction paper, and then hang them on a wall or door. Choose slides that seem interesting to your or your child or use these printed slides as a learning tool when completing an activity.

- Print the Emoticon and Acronym Cards (CD Supplement 8G) from the CD, cut them out, glue them to construction paper, and hang them in a creative manner on the wall. You will be ready for Activity 7: Emoticons and Acronyms Quiz.

- Design an interactive game by following these steps:

    1. Attach a small piece of Velcro to the edge of the front of each emoticon and acronym card. Tape these cards to the wall or a large poster board.

    2. Attach the other side of the Velcro to the back of the card that gives the meaning of the emoticons and acronyms.

    3. Have your child play a game where she must match the name of the emoticon or acronym to the correct card with the meaning of the emoticon or acronym using Velcro.

    You could use magnets instead of Velcro. Or your child could attach the cards using paperclips if you don't have Velcro or magnets.

- Dedicate a section of your house to learning about communicating using the Internet. Refer to the information located in that area of your home throughout this chapter. Use a banner or letter cutouts to spell out "Communicating Using the Internet," the topic of this chapter. Hang completed work in this area.

- Change the screensaver or the desktop background of your computer to a picture that represents something that your child will be learning in this chapter, such as an emoticon, an envelope representing e-mail, or a globe representing communication worldwide. Display a globe or a picture of the Earth to refer to throughout the chapter to create visual images reminding your child that the Internet spans the entire world.

# Vocabulary

Review the following terms with your child so that he or she can have a basic understanding of the vocabulary used in this chapter. You could also have your child write the definitions in the Communicating Using the Internet Vocabulary worksheet (CD Supplement 8N).

**acronym:** A group of capital letters formed using the first initial of a set of words.

**e-mail:** E-mail is short for electronic mail, the transmission of messages over communications networks.

**e-mail address:** An electronic postal address with a username and domain name. (Example: username@yahoo.com)

**e-mail client:** Software that allows you to create an account to send and receive e-mail messages. For example, Microsoft Outlook, Yahoo, AOL, or Gmail.

**e-mail etiquette:** Being kind and polite when typing and sending e-mail. Also called netiquette.

**e-mail server:** A computer used to send e-mail that works as an Internet post office.

**emoticon:** A symbol made using characters from the keyboard to express feelings online.

**instant messaging (IM):** Messages that are electronically exchanged with another person in real time, often using nicknames.

**instant messaging client:** Software that allows users to send and receive instant messages.

**recipient:** The person receiving the e-mail message.

**spam:** Unsolicited e-mail that is sent to many people at one time.

**videoconferencing:** Real time video and audio communication with two or more people in different locations over the Internet.

**VoIP (Voice over Internet Protocol):** Real time transmission of voice signals over the Internet. Often called Internet phone service.

# NETS•S Addressed

2. **Communication and Collaboration**

   Students use digital media and environments to communicate and work collaboratively, including at a distance, to support individual learning and contribute to the learning of others. Students:

   a. interact, collaborate, and publish with peers, experts, or others employing a variety of digital environments and media

   b. communicate information and ideas effectively to multiple audiences using a variety of media and formats

   c. develop cultural understanding and global awareness by engaging with learners of other cultures

   d. contribute to project teams to produce original works or solve problems

5. **Digital Citizenship**

   Students understand human, cultural, and societal issues related to technology and practice legal and ethical behavior. Students:

   a. advocate and practice the safe, legal, and responsible use of information and technology

   b. exhibit a positive attitude toward using technology that supports collaboration, learning, and productivity

   c. demonstrate personal responsibility for lifelong learning

   d. exhibit leadership for digital citizenship

# Grades

Think of the best way to determine your child's comprehension of this online communications chapter. This is your child's opportunity to demonstrate her individual understanding. Throughout each activity, evaluate your child while she works. When deciding on the type of assessment, consider your child's age and abilities and give clear expectations so that she understands all that is expected of her and that as a result she can be successful.

The following are some suggestions that might help you to assess your child.

- Use the answer keys in the various activities to grade the supplements that your child completed. Base the grades on accuracy or completion. The answer keys can be found on the CD.

- You may want to use the Grade Book located in Appendix A at the back of this book to record your child's assignments and grades. Keep a running record of your child's progress to determine comprehension and understanding of the content. Record these observations on paper or in the Grade Book.

- Ask your child to write down the definitions to the vocabulary words in this chapter using the Communicating Using the Internet Vocabulary worksheet (CD Supplement 8N).

- Observe and document her efforts while she is watching slide shows and taking notes. Have your child write a paragraph describing the importance of using ethical behavior when communicating online.

- Have your child print at least one of her e-mail messages from Activity 3 so that you can see that she correctly filled in all of the information that you required. This will also give your child the ability to see the e-mail message in a printed format, reminding her that e-mail is permanent. Remind her that once you send something, the other person can print it out and show it to anyone.

- Require your child to write some appropriate and inappropriate ways to use IM. Discuss the ramifications of using IM inappropriately. Have your child print out his IM conversations and check for use of emoticons and acronyms while chatting.

## Enrichment

After your child has completed the activities in this chapter continue some online communication excitement by challenging your child to complete another Internet communications activity. Choose one of these enrichment activities, or plan your own that will motivate and move your child to the next level while learning about Internet communications.

### E-mail

- Find an e-pal for your child and provide a few minutes at a scheduled time for your child to check and send e-mail with his e-pal. Create assignments on information that your child must find out from his e-pal, or give him a specific topic to write about. You may decide to ask a friend or family member to be an e-pal, or you could use a website such as www.epals.com to find an e-pal.

- Have your child research and then write a paragraph describing methods that malicious hackers use to find and open e-mail messages to gather personal information. This will help your child to see the importance of protecting himself when sending and opening e-mail messages. Ask your child to research various types of spam and phishing attacks and then share recent news stories on how people have been tricked. Have him write a report explaining the reason why junk e-mail messages are called spam.

- Communicate with your child using e-mail. Have your child check his e-mail to see your technology assignment for the day. Have your child research to discover when the first recorded e-mail was sent. Ask your child to explain the similarities and differences between instant messaging and e-mail messages. Have your child go online to locate e-mail etiquette techniques and make a list of the top 10 that he feels are the most important.

**Instant Messaging**

- Many websites now offer online assistance with real people sending and receiving instant messages to answer questions about products and services. Ask your child to think about this IM concept and explain whether this assistance is really helpful. Why or why not?

- Have your child research the various IM clients used to send and receive IM. Ask your child to pick a favorite and write down at least five reasons why it is his favorite. Have your child explain how to mark that you are "away" or "offline" when using IM.

- If you have two computers at your house, communicate with your child using IM, allowing your child to ask you questions or respond to you using IM. You could chat about a topic such as: What do you want for dinner? Or, what do you want to do for fun this weekend?

- Give your child an opportunity to go online and search for more emoticons and acronyms and make a list of his favorites. Ask your child to research how IM works using computers and servers and write a paragraph describing this process.

### VoIP and Videoconferencing

- Design an assignment that allows your child to communicate for a few months with another person in a different location using VoIP or videoconferencing. At a specific time, have your child call the person, talk with him or her, and ask specific questions about his or her town. Have your child keep a journal with notes about the person and then discuss what your child learned.

- Have your child research the possibility for hackers to listen to a VoIP phone call. How does the military or a company ensure that video communications are secure when communicating secret information? Have your child research to discover when the first videoconference was conducted.

- Have your child research electronic communication using satellites and then write a report explaining how an interplanetary Internet might work.

- Ask your child to research the plethora of online classes that are now offered using videoconferencing and write a paragraph explaining how videoconferencing works with the online class.

## Closure

Allow a few moments for your child to think about all she has learned in this chapter concerning online communications. This allows your child to process and reflect upon all that she has learned about e-mail, instant messaging, VoIP, and videoconferencing. The following are some suggestions for closure activities.

- Ask, "What have you learned about communicating online?" Encourage your child to share a few interesting facts or trivia that she has learned during this chapter. Encourage your child to share a story or personal experience concerning the concepts learned about the right and wrong way to communicate online.

- Allow your child to send you an e-mail message describing one thing that she has learned about communicating online.

Activity 1

# E-mail Slide Show

Easy to
Modify for
Younger Kids

## Goal

Your child will watch a slide show to learn about the following concepts: how e-mail works, e-mail clients, e-mail servers, e-mail addresses, e-mail etiquette, and spam.

## Materials

- E-mail Slide Show (CD Supplement 8A)
- computer
- paper and pencil

## Steps

### 1. Prepare

Open the E-mail Slide Show (CD Supplement 8A).
Click Slide Show > View Slide Show when you are ready to begin.

### 2. Learn

As you advance each slide, have your child read along with you to learn about the following concepts: how e-mail works, e-mail client, e-mail server, e-mail address, e-mail etiquette, and spam. Your child could tell you about any of the terms that he already knows while watching the slide show.

The slide show also includes some Internet safety concepts that are discussed in depth in Chapter 2: "Safety on the Internet." When reviewing the 10 Kids' Rules for Online Safety, stress the particular rules that correspond to e-mail such as number four: I will never send a person my picture or anything else without first checking with my parents.

## 3. Review

Play the slide show again and have your child recall each term to the best of his ability. Your child could advance the slides during the multimedia presentation.

## 4. Write

Your child should have a good understanding of these e-mail concepts and the correct way to behave when using e-mail. Instruct your child to take notes and write down the terms and definitions from the slide show.

**Tip**
Explain the similarities and differences in e-mail and "snail" (postal) mail. This will help prepare your child for the next few activities about e-mail.

Activity **2**

# *How E-mail Works*

## Goal

Your child will learn the basic procedures for writing and sending an e-mail message, and then complete a worksheet.

## Materials

- E-mail Procedures Worksheet (CD Supplement 8B)
- E-mail Procedures Worksheet Answers (CD Supplement 8C)
- paper and pencil

## Steps

### 1. Teach

Discuss how e-mail works by explaining the following general procedures for writing and sending an e-mail message. The procedures will be different depending on which e-mail client you will be using. Show your child this on your computer, or write it down on paper while discussing the procedures.

**Procedures for Writing and Sending an E-mail Message**

Have your child follow these steps:

1. Log into your e-mail client account. (E-mail client examples: Microsoft Outlook, Yahoo, AOL, Gmail)

2. Click Compose Mail or New Mail.

3. Fill in the Header.

   **To:** [Type the recipient's e-mail address.]

   **Subject:** [Type a short statement describing the message's content.]

   **CC:** [Type an e-mail address of anyone that you want to receive a copy of the message.]

**BCC:** [Type an e-mail address of anyone that you want to receive a copy of the message without anyone else seeing their e-mail address.]

4. Write your message in the large space provided. Don't use any private information, unless you encrypt it. Anyone can read your e-mail message when it is sent as clear or plain text (i.e., not encrypted) via the Internet. Remind your child to *never* send passwords, credit card numbers, or any other sensitive information via e-mail without first encrypting the data. Malicious hackers can easily see plain text and can obtain your information when you send it over the Internet.

5. Click Send.

## 2. Worksheet

Have your child put the steps to writing and sending an e-mail in the correct order on the E-mail Procedures Worksheet (CD Supplement 8B) by writing the correct number next to the corresponding step.

## 3. Check

Use the E-mail Procedures Worksheet Answers (CD Supplement 8C) to check and make sure that your child put the procedures in the correct order. Go over any missed answers so that your child understands the general procedures for sending an e-mail message.

**Tip**
Draw the "@" symbol on a piece of paper and discuss the differences between a website address (www.yahoo.com) and an e-mail address (username@yahoo.com).

Activity 3

# Send an E-mail

## Goal

Your child will write and then send an e-mail message.

## Materials

- E-mail Message Worksheet (CD Supplement 8D)
- computer with Internet access
- pencil

## Steps

### 1. Create

You may already have an e-mail account for your child; if not, you may decide to create one now, or your child could use your e-mail account for this activity. If you need to create an e-mail account, choose one of the popular free e-mail clients such as Gmail (http://mail.google.com), Hotmail (www.hotmail.com), or Yahoo (https://edit.yahoo.com/registration).

### 2. Write

Have your child fill in the recipient, subject, and your child's e-mail message on the E-mail Message Worksheet (CD Supplement 8D). Talk to your child about topics he could write about and the person he wants to send the message to, which could be another family member or a friend.

### 3. Check

Check the E-mail Message Worksheet (CD Supplement 8D) to make sure your child filled in the e-mail address and subject correctly. Also check for any grammatical errors in the body of the letter.

## 4. Send

Have your child log in to the e-mail account to type and send the message using the information from the worksheet.

## 5. Reply

If your child has a new message in his inbox, show him how to open the new message that he has received and then have him reply to that message.

**Tips**

Remind your child not to open any attachments if he doesn't know who sent them, unless he knows it is safe. It could be a virus that could harm his computer.

Discuss the different options associated with an e-mail message, such as High Importance, Low Importance, Flag, Font, Sent Mail, Drafts, Deleted Items, and Reply to All, and then allow your child to create and send another message using some of these new things.

Activity **4**

# Instant Messaging Slide Show

Easy to
Modify for
Younger Kids

## Goal

Your child will watch a slide show to learn about instant messaging.

## Materials

- Instant Messaging Slide Show (CD Supplement 8E)
- computer
- paper and pencil

## Steps

### 1. Prepare

Open the Instant Messaging Slide Show (CD Supplement 8E).
Click Slide Show > View Slide Show when you are ready to begin.

The slide show includes information on instant messaging, emoticons, and acronyms as well as a review of Internet safety concepts from Chapter 2: "Safety on the Internet." When reviewing the 10 Kids' Rules for Online Safety, stress the particular rules that correspond to instant messaging such as number one: I will not give out personal information such as my address, telephone number, parents' work address/ telephone number, or the name and location of my school without my parents' permission.

### 2. Learn

As you advance each slide, have your child read along with you to learn about instant messaging.

### 3. Review

Play the slide show again and have your child recall each term to the best of her ability. Your child could advance the slides during the multimedia presentation.

### 4. Write

Instruct your child to write down the definition of instant messaging and any other important notes from the slide show.

**Tips**

Instruct your child that she should never give out personal information, including her name, when using IM because it is not secure and anyone can read it. Children should take responsibility and be held accountable for the things that they write in any IM. Children should never talk to anyone that they don't know when using IM. Children should never meet in person anyone whom they've met only through IM.

Activity 5

# Send an Instant Message (IM)

## Goal

Your child will send and receive instant messages using a computer.

## Materials

- computer with Internet access

## Steps

### 1. Prepare

If you don't already have an IM client, you will need to conduct research using Google or a different search engine of your choice to locate one that you want to use for this activity. You will find many free instant messaging services. Others may require a small fee. Once you find one you like, download and install the client or server. Preview the site and become familiar with navigation.

Often, instant messaging environments are embedded in popular social networking websites, games, and business applications. In the case of embedded IM environments, you only need to allow a Java applet, Active X, Flash, or other control module to be installed into your web browser. There are also options that will allow you to use a client that is embedded within your web browser while still connecting to a remote server of your choice. Choose the option with which you are most comfortable. Here are a few instant messaging clients:

- AOL Instant Messenger (AIM, stand-alone and embedded client-server)
- Facebook (embedded)
- Meebo (embedded client-server)
- Google Talk (stand-alone)
- Pidgin (stand-alone)
- Trillian (stand-alone)
- Windows Live Messenger (stand-alone)
- Yahoo! Messenger (stand-alone)

## 2. Friend

Set up a time and day with a family member or friend who can be online at the same time and is willing to send and receive a few IMs. Choose a topic or allow your child to choose a topic for the conversation.

## 3. Send and Receive

Discuss and clearly show step-by-step how to send and receive an IM. Here's a sample procedure for your child to use for sending and receiving IMs:

1. Log into your IM account.

2. Click or type the screen name of the person you want to send a message to.

3. Type a message and click Send or press Enter.

4. Watch for the person to send a message back to you.

**Tip**
Remind your child that when you are talking to someone using IM, it is polite to continue the conversation. If you are unable to talk with the person, or if you need him to hold, then tell him you are logging off or ask him to hold so he is not waiting too long.

Activity **6**

# Emoticons and Acronyms Slide Show

Easy to Modify for Younger Kids

## Goal

Your child will learn the meaning of 10 emoticons and 10 acronyms using a slide show presentation.

## Materials

- Emoticons and Acronyms Slide Show (CD Supplement 8F)
- computer

## Steps

### 1. Prepare

Open the Emoticons and Acronyms Slide Show (CD Supplement 8F). Click Slide Show > View Slide Show when you are ready to begin.

### 2. Play

As you advance each slide, have your child read the meaning of the emoticons and acronyms while playing the slide show. For each emoticon, have your child act out or copy the expression during the slide show.

### 3. Draw

Play the slide show again and have your child draw an illustration for each emoticon using markers or crayons on paper. Replay the slide show a few times (if needed) and try to have your child memorize the emoticons and acronyms.

**Tips**

During the presentation, have your child write down any of the emoticons or acronyms that she doesn't know so she can practice these at a later time. Try to have your child practice all 20 emoticons and acronyms. Tell your child to repeat after you if she needs help saying the names. Have your child type the emoticons using different word processors, showing that some word processors automatically change the emoticon into an actual smiley face, while other simple word processors, such as Notepad, keep the original characters that your child types.

Activity 7

# Emoticons and Acronyms Quiz

## Goal

Your child will review the emoticons and acronyms using cards and then take a quiz.

## Materials

- Emoticon and Acronym Cards (CD Supplement 8G)
- Emoticons Quiz (CD Supplement 8H)
- Emoticons and Acronyms Quiz (CD Supplement 8I)
- Emoticons Quiz Answers (CD Supplement 8J)
- Emoticons and Acronyms Quiz Answers (CD Supplement 8K)
- pencil

## Steps

### 1. Prepare

Print and cut out the Emoticon and Acronym Cards (CD Supplement 8G). You may decide to print in black and white for older children if you want to make it more challenging to find the matching card. Cut each card so that the emoticon is separate from its meaning and the acronym is separate from its meaning. Glue the cards to construction paper for added durability.

### 2. Review

Show the emoticon or acronym card to your child and have him show you the matching card, or ask him to just say the meaning. For example, if you hold up the **:-)** card, then your child should hold up the card that says "happy."

### 3. *Quiz*

Decide which quiz will best meet the needs of your child, or assign both the Emoticons Quiz and the Emoticons and Acronyms Quiz (CD Supplements 8H and 8I). Explain the instructions at the top of the assessment. Give your child enough time to take the quiz to determine all that he has learned about emoticons and acronyms.

### 4. *Check*

Use the Emoticons Quiz Answers (CD Supplement 8J) and the Emoticons and Acronyms Quiz Answers (CD Supplement 8K) to grade your child's work. Go over any missed questions with your child.

**Tips**
Have your child use an emoticon or acronym in an e-mail or IM. For extra practice he could play a matching game with the learning cards where he needs to find the matches to all of the cards.

Activity 8

# VoIP and Videoconferencing Slide Show

Easy to
Modify for
Younger Kids

## Goal

Your child will watch a slide show on VoIP (Voice over Internet Protocol) and videoconferencing.

## Materials

- VoIP and Videoconferencing Slide Show (CD Supplement 8L)
- VoIP and Videoconferencing Worksheet (CD Supplement 8M)
- computer
- pencil

## Steps

### 1. Prepare

Open the VoIP and Videoconferencing Slide Show (CD Supplement 8L). Click Slide Show > View Slide Show when you are ready to begin.

### 2. Learn

As you advance each slide, have your child read along with you to learn about VoIP and videoconferencing. Your child could tell you about any of the terms that she already knows while watching the slide show.

The slide show also includes some Internet safety concepts that are discussed more in Chapter 2: "Safety on the Internet." When reviewing the 10 Kids' Rules for Online Safety, stress the particular rules that correspond to VoIP and Videoconferencing such as number nine: I will be a good online citizen and not do anything that hurts other people or is against the law.

### 3. Research

Have your child write three advantages and three disadvantages to using VoIP and videoconferencing and complete the VoIP and Video-conferencing Worksheet (CD Supplement 8M). If necessary, allow your child to research online to locate the advantages and disadvantages.

### 4. Discuss

Discuss the advantages and disadvantages of using VoIP and video-conferencing that your child wrote on the worksheet. Example: A significant advantage of using VoIP is the ability to make free local and long distance calls to cell phones, other VoIP phones, and regular phones. A vital disadvantage is the need for electricity and a good Internet connection to make a clear phone call.

**Tip**
To encourage Internet safety, ask your child to write down at least two Internet safety concepts to think about when communicating using VoIP and videoconferences.

Activity 9

# VoIP Phone Call

Easy to
Modify for
Younger Kids

## Goal

Your child will make a VoIP phone call to another person.

## Materials

* computer with microphone and speakers and high-speed Internet access, a special VoIP phone, or a VoIP adapter with a regular telephone
* pencil and paper

## Steps

### 1. Prepare

Before this activity, make a practice VoIP phone call to determine how you want to make the phone call so that you are familiar with the steps. You may need to install VoIP software, such as Skype. Plan a day and time with a friend or family member so that your child can call that person during this activity. If you need help setting up the VoIP phone call, the following sites have good information:

**Education World: Skype:**
www.educationworld.com/a_tech/techtorial/techtorial107.shtml

**How Stuff Works:**
http://communication.howstuffworks.com/ip-telephony.htm

**Skype:** www.skype.com

### 2. Call

Discuss how VoIP works by explaining the steps to making a phone call using the Internet. The following is the general procedure for making a VoIP phone call. More detailed steps may be added depending on the way you want to make the VoIP call in your home.

**Procedure for Making a VoIP Phone Call**

You may need to assist your child when completing the following steps to making a VoIP phone call. Allow your child to do as much as he is able to do depending on his age and abilities.

- Log onto a high-speed Internet connection using VoIP software, such as Skype.

- Decide which device you want to use to make a phone call over the Internet. Currently, there are three main ways to make a VoIP phone call: use a computer with microphone and speakers, use a special VoIP Phone, or use a VoIP adapter with a regular telephone.

- Call and talk to a friend using the VoIP or regular phone line. In most cases the other person does not need to have the same VoIP software to make a VoIP call; however, the software must use a compatible implementation of the VoIP protocol and be properly configured.

## 3. Write

After the VoIP phone call, have your child write a short paragraph explaining whether he liked or did not like the VoIP call, including reasons why or why not.

**Tips**

Talk about the similarities and differences in telephone calls using POTS (Plain Old Telephone System) and a telephone call using VoIP technology. If you have a VoIP phone, have your child tell you the similarities and differences of the VoIP phone and your regular home telephone.

Activity **10**

Easy to
Modify for
Younger Kids

# *Videoconference*

## Goal

Your child will videoconference with another person.

## Materials

- Webcam, built in laptop camera, or a video camera connected to your computer with Internet access
- pencil and paper

## Steps

### 1. Prepare

Plan a day and time with a friend or family member so that your child can videoconference with that person during this activity. It will be fun if the friend has a video camera, too! Before this activity, have a practice videoconference to make sure everything is set up correctly.

To set up your videoconference, you will need videoconferencing software or instant messaging software such as Yahoo. There are many ways to have a videoconference. If you need help setting up the videoconference, you may want to visit one of these pages for some information:

**eHow**

> **How to Hook Up a Video Conference Camera:** www.ehow.com/
> how_4598229_hook-up-video-conference-camera.html

> **How to Video Conference for Free:**
> www.ehow.com/how_4690016_video-conference-free.html

> **How to Set Up a Web Camera:**
> www.ehow.com/how_3879_set-web-camera.html

**How Stuff Works**

> **How Webcams Work:** http://computer.howstuffworks.com/webcam.htm

## 2. *Videoconference*

Discuss how videoconferencing works by explaining the tools needed to make a videoconference.

- Camera, webcam, or laptop with built-in camera
- Speakers
- Microphone
- Monitor or projector
- Videoconferencing software or instant messaging software such as Yahoo! or Windows Live Messenger
- Internet connection

The videoconference should probably take about 10–20 minutes, depending on the time restraints of the individuals in the conference and the attention spans of the children involved. The communication during the conference could be short and simple with questions such as "How are you?" and "What have you been doing today?" or it could be more thought-provoking with discussion questions such as "What is your favorite place to go on vacation?" or "How often do you videoconference?" Before the conference, your child could write down a few questions about a particular topic that she is currently learning about, such as insects or U.S. history, and then ask the other person the questions. For added fun, your child and the other person on the videoconference could sing a song together.

## 3. *Write*

After the videoconference, have your child write a short paragraph explaining whether she liked or did not like the videoconference, including reasons why or why not.

**Tips**

Have your child create a list of detailed steps to having a videoconference so it will be easy the next time you try it. If your child has already had several videoconferencing experiences, make it more challenging for her by having her ask the other person some specific questions or sharing a personal story about her favorite technology activity.

## Chapter 9

# Multimedia Presentations

## Objective

Children will be able to create and present a unique multimedia slide show by working through activities such as completing a word search, watching online stories and slide show tutorials, and using a storyboard to write and illustrate a story.

## Purpose

This chapter integrates creative writing with technology. Completing these activities will help children in their creative writing skills, expand their understanding of the Internet, and develop their multimedia capabilities. The chapter will acquire meaning when your child takes ownership of these concepts and feels that writing a story and creating a multimedia presentation are both worthwhile and important. Your child should feel a sense of achievement because your child's concepts will be taken from mere ideas to a beautiful animated slide show presentation.

# Activities Overview

This chapter will teach your child how to create a multimedia presentation through a variety of fun learning activities. Carefully consider which activities will benefit your child depending on his or her age, abilities, and learning styles. The following chart categorizes each activity to help you to plan the lessons. Some children may be able to complete all of them, whereas others would benefit by focusing more time on a few key activities. Certain children may require a more structured environment, whereas a self-motivated child could be given more freedom.

Remember, don't hurry to complete an activity just to have it completed. Your child should work at his or her own pace and really understand the concepts. You may want to repeat an activity, or allow your child more time on a certain activity such as Activity 7, when your child creates a slide show. Create a positive atmosphere while encouraging your child to learn with confidence. To get started, you may decide to plan a fun activity to inspire your child and focus your child's attention on multimedia presentations.

| Activities | Worksheet | Modifiable* | Internet Access | Game | Learning Cards | Slide Show | Arts and Crafts | Answer Key |
|---|---|---|---|---|---|---|---|---|
| 1. Online Stories | | ✔ | ✔ | | | | | |
| 2. Word Search | ✔ | | | ✔ | | | | ✔ |
| 3. Sample Slide Show | | ✔ | | | | ✔ | | |
| 4. Slide Show Tutorials | | | ✔ | | | | | |
| 5. Storyboard | ✔ | ✔ | | | | | | |
| 6. Storyboard Self-Assessment | ✔ | | | | | | | |
| 7. Create a Slide Show | | ✔ | | | | ✔ | | |
| 8. Rehearse | | ✔ | | | | ✔ | | |
| 9. Slide Show Presentation | ✔ | | | | | ✔ | | |
| 10. Make a Book | | ✔ | | | ✔ | | ✔ | |

* Easily modifiable for younger children

# CD Supplements

The following chart lists all of the CD supplements for this chapter and provides the CD filename, supplement title, and activity number. To make locating and using these supplements faster and easier, it is recommended that you copy all files to your hard drive before beginning the lessons.

| CD Filename | Title | Activity |
|:---:|:---|:---:|
| 9A | Multimedia Word Search | 2 |
| 9B | Multimedia Word Search Answers | 2 |
| 9C | My Counting Story | 3 |
| 9D | Counting Storyboard | 5 |
| 9E | Storyboard | 5 |
| 9F | Storyboard Self-Assessment | 6 |
| 9G | My Counting Story Template | 7 |
| 9H | Slide Show Template | 7 |
| 9I | Slide Show Assessment | 9 |
| 9J | Multimedia Presentations Vocabulary | Optional |

# Variations for Younger Children

This chapter provides a foundation for future multimedia presentations projects as well as future writing skills. You may need to shape the online stories and tutorials activities to meet your child's level of understanding. Feel free to modify the activities, such as removing a step, to meet the needs of your child. Monitor your child's expression to see if he is showing signs of frustration because the activity is too difficult or signs of boredom because the activity is too easy then modify the activity to help him succeed on his individual level. You could even make up your own activities. The following ideas may help.

- Assign a story topic such as counting or animals to simplify the writing process for younger children.

- It may be easier for younger children to write a counting story and use the Counting Storyboard and My Counting Story Template (CD Supplement 9D and 9G).

- Require younger children to create fewer slides, depending upon their ability.

- Read the online stories together with your child, especially if he is just learning to read. It would be best to locate online stories with audio if your child is still learning to read.

- Have your child navigate the online stories using his mouse while you read to him.

- Tell an imaginative counting story to motivate your child to think creatively before he begins writing his story.

- It may be easier for the younger child to type the word and insert the graphics for each slide at the same time, instead of typing all of the words first.

- Review the steps to creating a slide show several times and have your child repeat them to ensure comprehension. If the steps are repeated several times, your child will be able to visualize the process when he tries it.

- For a younger child, teach each step separately and have your child complete that step, rather than teaching all the steps at one time.

- Your child could choose one graphic for the entire counting story. Explain how to copy and paste that graphic onto the other slides. You may need to discuss that one graphic is on the first page, two graphics are on the second page, and continue in this manner to page 5, the last page.

- Advance the slides during the presentation for your child.

- Create a song to a familiar tune to teach the steps to creating a slide.

## Internet Safety

In this chapter, some activities require Internet access. Remind your child to think about Internet safety during these activities. You may want to review the Internet safety tips on pages 10–11.

## Fun Decorations

An inspiring room atmosphere and decorated walls will excite your children and focus their attention on multimedia presentations. Be creative in assembling decorations to motivate your children to learn about multimedia presentations. The following are some ideas that might help you with decorations.

- Dedicate a section of your house to learning about multimedia presentations. Refer to the information located in that area of your home throughout this chapter. Use a banner or letter cutouts to spell out "Multimedia Presentations," the topic of this chapter. Hang your child's completed work in this area. Hang up posters focusing on multimedia presentations.

- If you choose a topic for the stories, such as animals, seasons, holidays, poems, or sports, decorate the room using that theme. Change the desktop background to a screenshot of a popular children's book cover.

## Vocabulary

Review the following terms with your child so that he or she can have a basic understanding of the vocabulary used in this chapter. You could also have your child write the definitions in the Multimedia Presentations Vocabulary worksheet (CD Supplement 9J).

> **multimedia:** The integration of text, graphics, sound, and animation using a computer.

> **multimedia presentation:** A slide show that integrates text, graphics, sound, and animation.

## NETS•S Addressed

1. **Creativity and Innovation**

   Students demonstrate creative thinking, construct knowledge, and develop innovative products and processes using technology. Students:

   a. apply existing knowledge to generate new ideas, products, or processes

   b. create original works as a means of personal or group expression

   c. use models and simulations to explore complex systems and issues

   d. identify trends and forecast possibilities

# Grades

There are many ways to determine your child's comprehension of multimedia presentations. Give your child ample opportunities to excel through a variety of means. Your child will work hard by nature because he will want to achieve satisfaction by developing a fantastic slide show. When deciding on the type of assessment, consider his age and abilities. The following are some suggestions that might help you to assess your child.

- Have your child edit his work using the Storyboard Self-Assessment (CD Supplement 9F).

- Assess your child on specific requirements using the Slide Show Assessment (CD Supplement 9I).

- Use the answer keys in the various activities to grade the supplements that your child completed. Base the grades on accuracy or completion. The answer keys can be found on the CD.

- You may want to use the Grade Book located in Appendix A at the back of this book to record your child's assignments and grades.

- Keep a running record of your child's progress to determine his comprehension and understanding of the content. Record these observations on paper or in the Grade Book (Appendix A).

- Instruct your child to complete his individual stories on the storyboard. Evaluate him based on completion, grammar, and creativity.

- Observe your child as he creates his slide show presentation and demonstrates the steps to creating a slide show.

- Have your child print his slide show presentation for evaluation when it is complete.

- Grade your child on how well he was able to navigate his slides during the presentation.

# Enrichment

Think of ways to inspire your child to use the online learning skills as well as the multimedia technology skills learned during this chapter. This chapter will likely spark some creative writing skills as well. There are many fun and innovative ways to kindle that flame with enrichment ideas. A variety of challenging and motivating ideas are offered in the following list.

- Submit your child's story to a writing contest.

- Encourage your child to write a sequel to her story.

- Have your child search the Internet for more online stories. This may result in the discovery of an interesting writing topic.

- Make several copies of the presentation, laminate the pages, and make them into books using comb binding. Distribute these books to family and friends as gifts.

- Encourage your child to make a slide show using her favorite nursery rhyme, poem, or cooking recipe.

- Create learning slide shows to help your child learn the alphabet, multiplication facts, shapes, colors, countries, or any other skills.

- Have your child create an additional slide show just for fun with few or no guidelines. This gives your child a chance to be creative and attempt new procedures. One suggestion is for your child to create a presentation describing herself or her family.

- Have your child use different multimedia software such as Hyper-Studio or Kid Pix (both available at www.mackiev.com) to create other multimedia presentations.

## Closure

Your child should feel a sense of accomplishment at the completion of creating the multimedia slide show presentations. Praise your child for having succeeded with such a big task. Think about a way to close this chapter with encouragement and praise for all the accomplished work. The following are some suggestions for closure activities.

- Encourage your child to share one thing he has learned while viewing the tutorials online.

- Ask your child to share his favorite part of creating a slide show.

- Encourage your child to explain a few concepts that he has learned about writing a story.

- Have your child think of another creative story topic that he would like to write about.

- Create and give your child a certificate for creating a multimedia presentation.

Activity **1**

# Online Stories

Easy to
Modify for
Younger Kids

## Goal

Your child will read and listen to online stories.

## Materials

- computer with Internet access

## Steps

### 1. Prepare

Listed below are several websites for children to read stories online. Become familiar with the websites ahead of time so that you can decide which sites are geared toward your child's reading level and interests.

**Ant Bee's Children's Stories:** www.antbee.com

**Children's Storybooks Online:** www.magickeys.com/books

**Fairy Tales:** http://fairytales.pppst.com

**Online Children's Stories:** www.ucalgary.ca/~dkbrown/stories.html

**The Real Mother Goose:** www.fidella.com/trmg/contents.html

### 2. Show

Show your child how he can navigate and read online stories by clicking the links or scrolling on the page.

### 3. Read

Allow your child to read and navigate the various stories on his own. You may decide to read the story to him while he navigates the pages. While reading the online stories, encourage your child to think about creative topics that he could use to create his own story.

## 4. Favorite

Encourage your child to share a favorite online story and the reason he liked the story. Have your child share a story idea that he might want to use for his multimedia slide show. Children will be writing their own stories in Activity 5.

Activity **2**

# Word Search

## Goal

Your child will learn the definition of multimedia while searching for words in a word search.

## Materials

- Multimedia Word Search (CD Supplement 9A)
- Multimedia Word Search Answers (CD Supplement 9B)
- pencil

## Steps

### 1. Prepare

Print the Multimedia Word Search (CD Supplement 9A).

### 2. Definition

Discuss the definition of multimedia with your child.

### 3. Check

Use the Multimedia Word Search Answers (CD Supplement 9B) to check the word search.

**Tip**
Allow your child to create her own word search on other slide show terms, such as slide show, art, presentation, insert, save, and file.

Activity **3**

# Sample Slide Show

Easy to Modify for Younger Kids

## Goal

Your child will watch and discuss particular aspects of a multimedia presentation.

## Materials

- My Counting Story (CD Supplement 9C)
- computer

## Steps

### 1. Open

Open the My Counting Story slide show (CD Supplement 9C). Click Slide Show > View Slide Show when you are ready to begin.

### 2. Read

Read the slide show along with your child.

### 3. Questions

Play the slide show again and ask these questions throughout the presentation.

- Where is the text?
- When do you hear sound?
- What is a graphic?
- When do you see animation?
- What did you like about this presentation?
- What would you change about this presentation?

Activity 4

# *Slide Show Tutorials*

## Goal

Your child will view an online tutorial to learn about creating multimedia presentations and then practice a few of these skills.

## Materials

- computer with Internet access
- paper and pencil
- multimedia presentation software (Microsoft PowerPoint or OpenOffice Impress Presentation)

## Steps

### *1. Prepare*

Listed below are several online tutorials for Microsoft PowerPoint and OpenOffice Impress Presentations. Choose the one that will be the best for your child's age and abilities. Become familiar with the website ahead of time, so you will know how to navigate the site. Your child could use more than one tutorial.

**Microsoft PowerPoint Tutorials**

**ActDen PowerPoint in the Classroom:** www.actden.com/pp/

**Education World PowerPoint Tutorial:**
www.educationworld.com/a_tech/tutorials/ew_ppt.htm

**Internet For Classrooms Microsoft PowerPoint:**
www.internet4classrooms.com/on-line_PowerPoint.htm

**PowerPoint Tutorial:**
http://oregonstate.edu/instruction/ed596/ppoint/pphome.htm

### OpenOffice Impress Presentation Tutorials

**About.com OpenOffice Impress:**

http://presentationsoft.about.com/od/openofficeimpress/
tp/071021openoffice_beginguide.htm  *—and—*

http://presentationsoft.about.com/od/openofficeimpress/Open_Office_
Impress_Free_Presentation_Software.htm

**LearnOpenOffice.org:** www.learnopenoffice.org/contents.htm

**OpenOffice.org Impress Tutorial:** http://documentation.openoffice.org/
tutorials/cospa/Cospa_Impress_Tutorial.pdf

**Tutorials for OpenOffice:**
www.tutorialsforopenoffice.org/category_index/presentation.html

**OpenOffice.org Impress In Pictures:** http://inpics.net/impress.html

## 2. Tutorial

Allow your child to complete the online tutorial, or just have her complete the sections that you want to focus on with her. You could have your child take notes from the site or complete any questions or quizzes during the tutorial.

## 3. Share

Have your child share some interesting facts learned while viewing the tutorial.

## 4. Practice

Show your child how to open the multimedia presentation software, Microsoft PowerPoint or OpenOffice Impress Presentation, on your computer. If needed, download and install the free OpenOffice Impress Presentation software. Allow your child to try a few skills that she has learned during the tutorial.

Activity **5**

# Storyboard

Easy to
Modify for
Younger Kids

## Goal

Your child will write a unique and creative story using a storyboard.

## Materials

- Counting Storyboard (CD Supplement 9D)
- Storyboard (CD Supplement 9E)
- pencil

## Steps

### 1. Topic

Allow time for your child to think about a topic and story to write. He may need to share ideas with you or write them on a piece of paper. Remind your child that the online stories may not be copied word for word because of copyright laws. If your child is having difficulty deciding on a topic, ask questions to inspire creativity.

### 2. Write

Give your child a few minutes to write down his ideas on a piece of blank paper. He can refer back to this when writing his story on the storyboard.

### 3. Storyboard

Your child will write his story on the Counting Storyboard or Storyboard (CD Supplement 9D or 9E). Choose the one that is best for your child. Specify the number of pages to include in the storyboard or allow your child to decide on the number of pages to include.

For younger children, allow your child to create a counting story using the Counting Storyboard (CD Supplement 9D). Have your child write a word in the blank and draw the number of items corresponding to the number on the page. For example, your child may write "apples" on the blank and draw three apples.

Explain to your child that the illustrations should be drawn in the box and the corresponding sentences should be written on the lines using the Storyboard (CD Supplement 9E).

**Tips**

Show your child the cover and title page of a book. Explain that the title of the book and the author's name appear on the cover of the book. Refer to the storyboard and explain that the title page is the same as the cover of a book.

Write some words on a piece of paper or create a word list to ensure correct spelling of frequently used words when your child begins writing. Have children's dictionaries available for your child to use when writing the story.

For fun, have your child write a few sentences about himself (the author) to include on the title page.

Assign your child to write a particular type of story such as fiction, nonfiction, explanatory, narrative, or persuasive when writing his story.

Activity **6**

# Storyboard Self-Assessment

## Goal

Your child will check her storyboard while completing a worksheet.

## Materials

- Storyboard Self-Assessment (CD Supplement 9F)
- completed storyboard from Activity 5
- pencil

## Steps

### 1. Read

Allow you child to read her storyboard and make any corrections needed.

### 2. Storyboard

Have your child read her storyboard again and use the Storyboard Self-Assessment (CD Supplement 9F) to make sure everything is correct. She will check her storyboard for accuracy using the checklist on this sheet. It may help to have your child start from her last page and work backwards to find any missed grammatical or syntax errors.

### 3. Check

Read your child's story, check for grammatical errors, and make any corrections needed.

Activity 7

# Create a Slide Show

Easy to
Mcdify for
Younger Kids

## Goal

Your child will create a multimedia slide show.

## Materials

- My Counting Story Template (CD Supplement 9G)
- Slide Show Template (CD Supplement 9H)
- completed storyboard from Activity 5
- computer with multimedia presentation software
  (Microsoft PowerPoint or OpenOffice Impress Presentation)

## Steps

### 1. New

To begin, open a Slide Show Template (CD Supplement 9G or 9H) or create a new presentation. Show your child how to save his file. Figures 9.1 and 9.2 illustrate menu choices for creating and saving presentations.

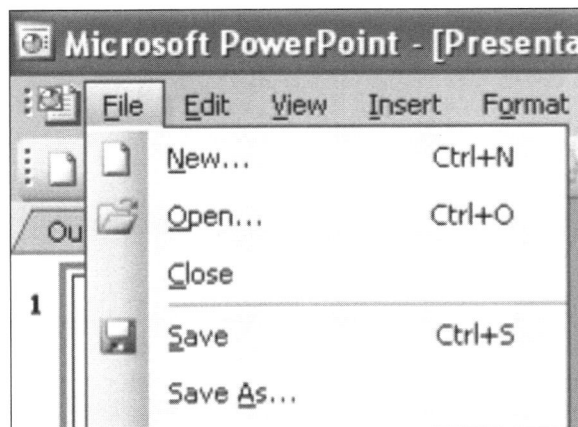

**Figure 9.1** Creating and saving a new presentation using Microsoft PowerPoint

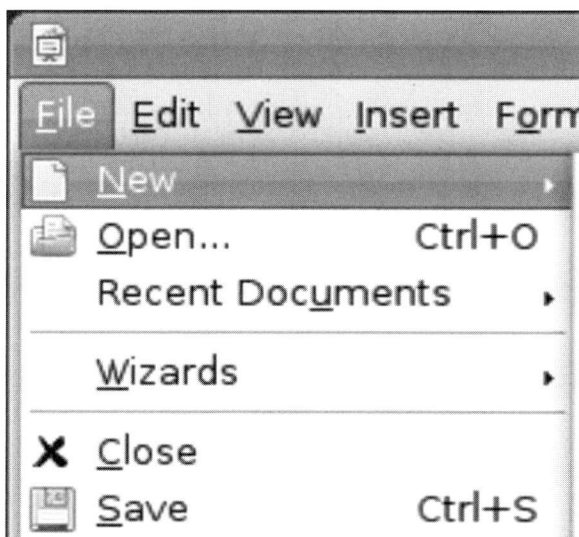

**Figure 9.2** Creating and saving a new presentation using OpenOffice Impress Presentation

## 2. Title

Have your child create the title page using his storyboard. It should include the title and the author's name. A graphic is optional. For fun, you could upload a digital picture of your child and include it on the title page.

## 3. Text

Instruct your child to type all the sentences from his storyboard using text or word art. Have him consider the font size and style to create a story that flows when reading.

## 4. Graphics

Direct your child to insert graphics to illustrate each page. The graphics should flow to create a meaningful story. For example, if your child has written a story about a bird learning to fly, each page should have a graphic with the same type of bird. The pages should look well proportioned and the pictures should fill up the entire page. Show some pages of a book to illustrate this point. You may decide to show your child the process of going on the Internet to locate a certain graphic. If your child is using the same graphic on several pages, it will be easier for him if you show him how to copy and paste the graphic. Figures 9.3 and 9.4 illustrate menu choices for inserting graphics.

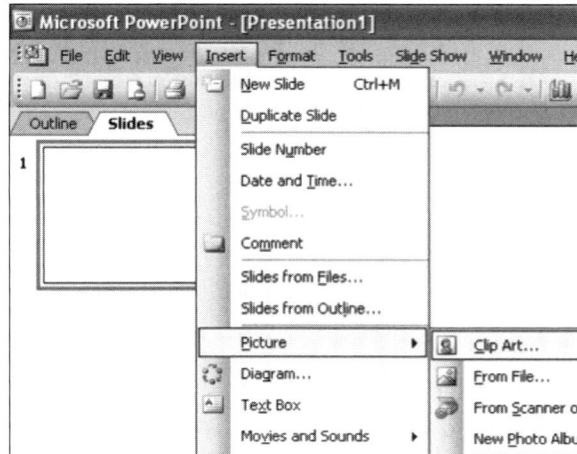

**Figure 9.3** Inserting graphics using Microsoft PowerPoint

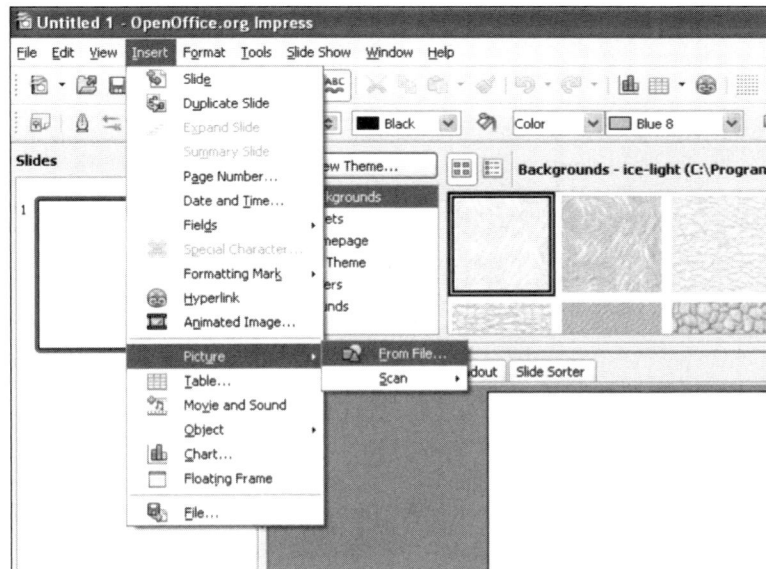

**Figure 9.4** Inserting graphics using OpenOffice Impress Presentation

## 5. Multimedia

Include multimedia effects (animations, transitions, sounds, and backgrounds). Instruct your child to animate at least one graphic or text on each slide. If needed, develop guidelines for the amount and type of multimedia elements added to the presentation. You may want to read your child's sentences and look at his graphics for accuracy before adding multimedia effects to the presentation to make sure everything looks correct.

**Tips**

There are different ways to create a slide show other than the steps discussed in this activity. If your child knows a shortcut or a different way to complete a step, let him show you. Refer to the online tutorials in Activity 4 if you need extra assistance. If needed, use the Help feature in PowerPoint or OpenOffice Impress Presentation while working. Remind your child to save often while working.

Activity 8

# *Rehearse*

## Goal

Your child will rehearse her multimedia slide show.

## Materials

- saved multimedia presentation from Activity 7
- computer with multimedia presentation software

## Steps

### *1. Open*

Have your child open her saved multimedia presentation created in Activity 7.

### *2. Review*

Discuss any slide show presentation techniques that you will be assessing during your child's presentation so your child will know all that is expected of her while she is presenting. Ask your child to explain the proper presentation practices back to you. You may want to review the following presentation practices.

- Speak in a clear, strong voice.
- Be lively when reading.
- Practice reading your story.
- Stand up straight.
- Be confident.
- Be familiar with the way to navigate your slide show.

### *3. Rehearse*

Allow your child to play her slide show and read each page aloud. Show your child how to advance the slides by herself. Your child should feel secure when sharing her story. This is a time for your child to show her personality. Give your child plenty of time to rehearse her slides; this should help her feel more assured.

Activity 9

# Slide Show Presentation

## Goal

Your child will present his multimedia slide show.

## Materials

- Slide Show Assessment (CD Supplement 9I)
- saved multimedia presentation
- computer with multimedia presentation software (Microsoft PowerPoint or OpenOffice Impress Presentation)

## Steps

### 1. Prepare

Open the slide show using the multimedia presentation software on your computer.

### 2. Discuss

Remind your child of the assessment sheet that you will be using during the presentation. Share your enthusiasm with your child and watch it spread as he anticipates presenting his story.

### 3. Presentation

Have your child present his slide show to a friend or another family member. The atmosphere should be accepting and non-threatening, allowing your child to feel self-assured. Use the Slide Show Assessment (CD Supplement 9I) to assess your child during the presentation.

Activity **10**

# Make a Book

Easy to
Modify for
Younger Kids

## Goal

Your child will print and decorate her slide show to make a book.

## Materials

- saved multimedia presentation
- computer with multimedia presentation software (Microsoft PowerPoint or OpenOffice Impress Presentation)
- printer
- paper for printer
- scissors (optional)
- stapler, hole punch, ribbon, comb binding (options for binding)
- markers, colored pencils, crayons, stickers, glitter, paint (optional)

## Steps

### 1. Open

Open the slide show using the multimedia presentation software on your computer.

### 2. Print

Have your child decide upon the size of book that she would like to create. She may even decide to make one large book and one small book. Have her experiment with printing six slides per page or use other printing options. You may suggest printing in black and white so your child can color the pictures on her own. Also, consider not printing the backgrounds or changing the background to white to save ink on your printer.

### 3. Bind

Have your child cut the pages if needed. She may also use a hole punch and ribbon, a stapler or comb binding (available at some printing stores) to bind the pages together.

### 4. Decorate

Allow your child to decorate each page using markers, colored pencils, crayons, stickers, glitter, and paint. She may decide to draw in her own illustrations.

### 5. Read

Have your child read the book to you or someone else.

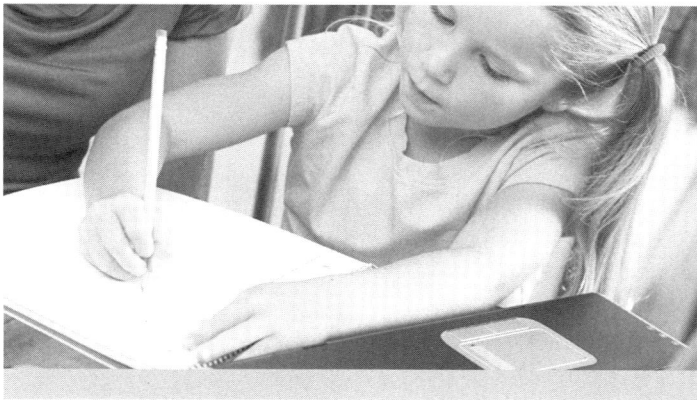

## Chapter 10

# Graphs and Spreadsheets

## Objective

Children will produce several creative graphs using a computer spreadsheet application and learn many skills such as sorting and creating formulas.

## Purpose

Provide personal meaning about graphs and spreadsheets to your children by encouraging them to take ownership of the information so that they will be committed to learning. Discuss the importance of knowing how to create graphs and use spreadsheets for school assignments and for life. Show that graphs are frequently used in newspapers and magazines, and being able to interpret the information is an important life skill. Explain that in this chapter they will learn how to use a spreadsheet application for calculating numbers and creating graphs. Encourage your children to really focus on this chapter and learn all that they can about graphs and spreadsheets!

# Activities Overview

The activities in this chapter offer many ways to learn and increase skills using a spreadsheet. The following chart categorizes each activity to help you to plan the lessons.

To get started, you may decide to plan a fun activity to inspire your child and focus his or her attention on graphs and spreadsheets. Encourage your child to share examples of occasions when graphs are used at school or in the community. Show a sample graph found in the newspaper or in a magazine. Ask your child to explain how graphs are important.

| Activities | Worksheet | Modifiable* | Internet Access | Game | Learning Cards | Slide Show | Arts and Crafts | Answer Key |
|---|---|---|---|---|---|---|---|---|
| **1.** Graph Slide Show | | ✔ | | | | ✔ | ✔ | |
| **2.** Graph Worksheet | ✔ | | ✔ | | | | | ✔ |
| **3.** Draw a Graph | ✔ | ✔ | | | | | ✔ | |
| **4.** Create a Graph Online | | ✔ | ✔ | | | | ✔ | |
| **5.** Spreadsheets | | ✔ | | ✔ | | | | |
| **6.** Spreadsheet Tutorials | | | ✔ | | | | | |
| **7.** Graphing with a Spreadsheet | | | | | | | ✔ | |
| **8.** Formulas | | ✔ | | | | | | |
| **9.** Sorting | | | | | | | | |
| **10.** Quiz | ✔ | ✔ | | | ✔ | | | ✔ |

* Easily modifiable for younger children

# CD Supplements

The following chart lists all of the CD supplements for this chapter and provides the CD filename, supplement title, and activity number. To make locating and using these supplements faster and easier, it is recommended that you copy all files to your hard drive before beginning the lessons.

| CD Filename | Title | Activity |
|---|---|---|
| 10A | Graph Slide Show | 1 |
| 10B | Graph Worksheet | 2 |
| 10C | Graph Worksheet Answers | 2 |
| 10D | Data Collection Worksheet | 3 |
| 10E | Bar Graph Worksheet | 3 |
| 10F | Graph and Spreadsheet Cards | 10 |
| 10G | Graphs and Spreadsheets Quiz I | 10 |
| 10H | Graphs and Spreadsheets Quiz II | 10 |
| 10I | Graphs and Spreadsheets Quiz I Answers | 10 |
| 10J | Graphs and Spreadsheets Quiz II Answers | 10 |
| 10K | Graphs and Spreadsheets Vocabulary | Optional |

# Variations for Younger Children

Children are able to create and explore spreadsheets at an early age because computers are readily available to them. Prepare appropriate activities that will allow younger children to explore ideas while giving them sufficient exposure to graphs and spreadsheets. Feel free to modify the activities, such as removing a step, to meet the needs of your child. Monitor your child's expression to see if he is showing signs of frustration because the activity is too difficult or signs of boredom because the activity is too easy then modify the activity to help him succeed on his individual level. You could even make up your own activities.

The following ideas may help.

- Concentrate on a few of the spreadsheets skills, instead of teaching all of the skills that are discussed throughout the chapter. You may want to expose your child to all of the skills, but focus on one or two at a time.

- Use a central theme based on something that your child is currently learning, such as holidays, food, families, or countries. This will allow your child to work with familiar concepts while learning about graphs.

- Design a graph together with your child using everyday activities to show your child that graphs represent real data. The following ideas may help.

  - Record how much exercise your child gets each day for one week.

  - Record how many hours your child sleeps each night for one week.

  - Record the amount of water your child drinks each day for one week.

- Go on a nature hunt to collect different-sized leaves or other nature items to be used to create a graph. Draw three columns on a piece of paper. If your child collected leaves, he could place the small leaves in the first column, and the medium-sized leaves in the second column, and attach the large leaves in the last column. Then, discuss with your child which column had the most or fewest leaves.

# Internet Safety

In this chapter, some activities require Internet access. Remind your child to think about Internet safety during these activities. You may want to review the Internet safety tips on pages 10–11.

# Fun Decorations

Do something different at your house for this chapter by creating an environment that will excite your child about graphs and spreadsheets. Decorations can generate enthusiasm as well as provide another opportunity to teach your child. Be inventive as you plan the room decorations, and remember to have fun! The following are some ideas that might help you with decorations.

- Print the slides from the Graph Slide Show (CD Supplement 10A), staple them to brightly colored construction paper, and display them in your home.

- Dedicate a section of your house to learning about graphs and spreadsheets. Refer to the information located in that area of your home throughout this chapter. Use a banner or letter cutouts to spell out "Graphs and Spreadsheets," the topic of this chapter. Hang completed work in this area.

- Cut out several different types of graphs from magazines and newspapers or print them from websites. Hang them on the wall or door and refer to them throughout the chapter.

- Change the screensaver or the desktop background of your computer to a picture that represents something that your child will be learning in this chapter, such as a graph.

- Make up a theme to concentrate on for the entire chapter such as exercising or healthy eating. As you work through each activity, incorporate facts from your theme so your child is learning about another topic while learning about graphing.

- Create a large graph on the wall that includes information about all of the members of your family. You could use poster board, cardboard, large construction paper, markers, paint, or other items to design the graph. Think of a fun topic to chart, such as favorite foods, amount of exercising done everyday, amount of television watched, the length of time it takes to complete homework, the amount of time spent on the phone, daily computer usage, or another topic that interests your child. You could record the data for a week or even a month. This is a great way to show that graphs represent real data.

# Vocabulary

Review the following terms with your child so that he or she can have a basic understanding of the vocabulary used in this chapter. You could also have your child write the definitions in the Graphs and Spreadsheets Vocabulary worksheet (CD Supplement 10K).

**bar graph:** Rectangular bars are used to show different values.

**cell:** A specific box on the grid, which is the intersection of a row and a column, such as A4 or D22.

**formula:** A mathematical equation that defines how the numbers in specific cells should be calculated.

**graph:** A diagram used to represent data.

**line graph:** Uses points connected by lines to show changes over time.

**pictograph:** A graph that uses pictures to represent values and ideas.

**pie chart:** A circular graph that is divided into sectors with each sector representing data.

**scatter diagram:** A graph with plotted points.

**spreadsheet:** A computer program with a grid of columns and rows that allows the user to input numbers and text.

# NETS•S Addressed

4. **Critical Thinking, Problem Solving, and Decision Making**

   Students use critical-thinking skills to plan and conduct research, manage projects, solve problems, and make informed decisions using appropriate digital tools and resources. Students:

   a.  identify and define authentic problems and significant questions for investigation

   b.  plan and manage activities to develop a solution or complete a project

    c.   collect and analyze data to identify solutions and make informed decisions

    d.   use multiple processes and diverse perspectives to explore alternative solutions

# Grades

Your child will have many opportunities to show all she has learned about graphs and spreadsheets in this chapter. Clearly explain throughout the chapter all that is expected of her. Your child's previous knowledge of graphs and spreadsheets may be considered when deciding the assessment method. Determine a way to authentically evaluate your child based on her individual accomplishments and creative abilities. The following are some suggestions that might help you to assess your child.

- Use the answer keys in the various activities to grade the supplements that your child completed. Base the grades on accuracy or completion. The answer keys can be found on the CD.

- You may want to use the Grade Book located in Appendix A at the back of this book to record your child's assignments and grades.

- Keep a running record of your child's progress to determine comprehension and understanding of the content. Record these observations on paper or in the Grade Book (Appendix A).

- Ask your child to write down the definitions for the vocabulary words in this chapter using the Graphs and Spreadsheets Vocabulary worksheet (CD Supplement 10K). This could be graded.

- Observe your child while she is searching, viewing, and interpreting data for graphs. Record these observations on a piece of paper or in the Grade Book.

- Have your child print some of the graphs and turn them in to you for a grade. Check for specific items on the graphs that were required, such as the title, labels, and data. If your child is unable to print the graph, look at the monitor to assess the graph.

- Assess your child when she takes the quizzes that are a part of the online tutorials.

- Direct your child to submit any data collected to create the graph. If your child got information from a website, require her to submit the URL (uniform resource locator).

# Enrichment

Your child may be excited about graphing and spreadsheets and want to create more elaborate graphs and collect data on interesting topics. If so, provide opportunities for him to build upon the graphs and spreadsheets skills learned in this chapter. Think of your own activities or choose a few of the following activities to encourage your child to go beyond all that was learned about spreadsheets and graphs.

- Encourage your child to practice different spreadsheet skills that were not discussed in this chapter such as inserting a new sheet, changing font colors and cell colors, adding numbers using Auto Sum, modifying the borders, inserting an auto filter, modifying the width and height of a cell, or wrapping text within a cell.

- Encourage your child to work through the tutorials again to practice as well as learn more graphs and spreadsheets skills.

- Have your child research the differences between Microsoft Excel and OpenOffice Calc and list the advantages and disadvantages of these spreadsheets.

- Ask your child to create a line graph on the number of fruit servings he eats each day for a week. Then create a bar graph or pictograph to show the data.

- Encourage your child to research online to locate and list different types of graphs that were not discussed in this chapter.

- Have your child collect data and create a graph based on his interests and hobbies, such as baseball, swimming, or music.

- Instruct your child to copy and paste a graph into a word processing document and then write a paragraph interpreting the results of the data portrayed in the graph.

- Use other graphing software and educational applications to demonstrate graphing, such as The Graph Club by Tom Snyder Productions (www.tomsnyder.com).

- Have your child go online to view graphs showing Internet usage around the world. A good source is Internet World Stats (www. internetworldstats.com/stats.htm).

- Allow your child to check his math homework using formulas in a spreadsheet.

- Have your child write down all of the vocabulary terms and definitions in a spreadsheet and then sort them in ascending order using the Sort icon.

- Have your child create a monthly budget using a spreadsheet.

- Encourage your child to use the spreadsheet to type and practice the multiplication tables.

- Have your child create formulas that reference other cells using a spreadsheet. For example, tell your child: "Type a formula into cell D3 that equals 10." Your child could type 5 in D1 and 5 in D2 and then a formula such as =*D1+D2* in cell D3.

- Have your child create a graph using the spreadsheet without any assistance.

## Closure

Promote a sense of accomplishment at the completion of the chapter. Allow a few moments for your child to contemplate all that she has learned about graphs and spreadsheets. The following are some suggestions for closure activities.

- Ask, "What have you learned about graphs and spreadsheets?" Encourage your child to share a few interesting facts or trivia that she has learned during this chapter.

- Ask your child to discuss her favorite type of graph.

Activity **1**

# Graph Slide Show

Easy to
Modify for
Younger Kids

## Goal

Your child will watch a slide show and learn about five different types of graphs and definitions.

## Materials

- Graph Slide Show (CD Supplement 10A)
- computer
- paper and pencil
- markers, crayons, or colored pencils

## Steps

### 1. Prepare

Open the Graph Slide Show (CD Supplement 10A).
Click Slide Show > View Slide Show when you are ready to begin.

### 2. Learn

As you advance each slide, have your child read along with you to learn the definitions of five different types of graphs: line graph, bar graph, pictograph, pie chart, and scatter diagram. Your child could also describe differences and similarities in the graphs.

### 3. Review

Show the slide show again and have your child recall the definitions before they appear on the screen. Your child could advance the slides during the multimedia presentation.

## 4. Draw

Have your child choose one type of graph from the slide show to copy and then illustrate on paper. Allow him to decorate his paper with markers, crayons, or colored pencils.

**Tips**
Instruct your child to find different types of graphs in a newspaper or magazine and describe the graphs. This will show him that there are many different types of graphs. Ask your child to explain how graphs allow us to visually see data, so he will understand that a graph represents real information.

Activity **2**

# Graph Worksheet

## Goal

Your child will view graphs online and then sketch and write the meanings of five different types of graphs on a worksheet.

## Materials

- Graph Worksheet (CD Supplement 10B)
- Graph Worksheet Answers (CD Supplement 10C)
- computer with Internet access
- pencil

## Steps

### 1. Prepare

Listed below are two sites that include sample graphs. Choose the one that will be the best for your child's age and abilities. Become familiar with the website ahead of time, so you will know how to navigate the site.

**NetCharts Chart Gallery:**
www.visualmining.com/resource_library/gallery/gallery.html

**ZedGraph: Sample Graphs:**
http://zedgraph.org/wiki/index.php?title=Sample_Graphs

### 2. Worksheet

As your child views the graphs online, she should fill in the information on the Graph Worksheet (CD Supplement 10B). She will sketch each type of graph that she finds and write a definition using her own words.

## 3. Check

Use the Graph Worksheet Answers (CD Supplement 10C) to check your child's work. Go over any missed items.

**Tips**
If needed, allow your child to view the slide show again to write the definitions in the blanks. While your child is viewing the graphs online, discuss how to interpret the meaning of the graph. Allow your child to draw a sketch of different types of graphs that she finds interesting on a separate piece of paper.

Activity **3**

# Draw a Graph

## Goal

Your child will collect data by surveying 10 people, and then draw a bar graph to represent the data.

## Materials

- Data Collection Worksheet (CD Supplement 10D)
- Bar Graph Worksheet (CD Supplement 10E)
- markers, crayons, or colored pencils

## Steps

### 1. Data

Have your child complete the Data Collection Worksheet (CD Supplement 10D) by writing five types of fruit in the first column, asking 10 different people about their favorite fruit, making tallies, and then writing the totals in the third column.

### 2. Graph

Have your child use the data from Step 1 to fill in the Bar Graph Worksheet (CD Supplement 10E). Your child should write in the types of fruit on the bottom and draw a line across each column to indicate the number of people who chose that as their favorite fruit.

### 3. Color

Ask your child to use markers, crayons, or colored pencils to color the bars. Each bar should be a different color.

**Tip**
Allow your child to choose a different topic, gather data, and then create another graph on a poster board.

Activity 4

# Create a Graph Online

## Goal

Your child will group objects and then create a graph online.

## Materials

- set of objects (see examples in Step 1)
- pencil and paper
- computer with Internet access
- printer
- paper for printer
- markers, crayons, or colored pencils (optional)

## Steps

### 1. Prepare

Listed below are two good examples of chart creation websites. Choose the one that will be best for your child's age and abilities. Become familiar with the website ahead of time so you will know how to navigate the site and be able to help your child use the tool. You may want to allow your child to use both sites.

**Chart Tool:** www.onlinecharttool.com/graph.php

**Kids' Zone: Create a Graph:** http://nces.ed.gov/nceskids/graphing/

Decide on an exciting set of objects for your child to sort and count. This data will be used to create her graph. Think of some items you have around the house or choose a set from the following list.

- assorted shapes (triangles, squares, circles, etc.)
- colored candy (Skittles or M&Ms)
- colored blocks
- Lego building bricks
- colored rubber bands
- colored toothpicks

## 2. Data

Have your child put the different colors or shapes into groups. Next, she should count the piles of items, and that will be her data for the graph. Instruct your child to record her data on paper to be used to create the graph. For example, if she was using a bag of M&Ms, her data may be "green–5, brown–10, red–2, yellow–8, and orange–3."

## 3. Create

Have your child follow the steps on the chart creation website to create a graph online. First, your child should choose which type of graph to create. Then she can design the graph, insert data, create labels, and preview her graph.

## 4. Print

Allow your child to print her graph.

## 5. Decorate

Provide markers, crayons or colored pencils for your child to color the different sections of the graph. You could display the graph in your home.

**Tip**
For extra practice, you could require your child to create a different type of graph using the website.

Activity **5**

# *Spreadsheets*

## Goal

Your child will learn the definitions of spreadsheet and cell and play a game.

## Materials

- computer
- spreadsheet program (Microsoft Excel or OpenOffice Calc)

## Steps

### 1. Prepare

Show your child how to open Microsoft Excel or OpenOffice Calc. If needed, download and install the free spreadsheet named Calc from OpenOffice.org before you begin.

### 2. Rows and Columns

Allow your child to open a new spreadsheet and click around in the different cells. Show him the letters along the columns at the top of the spreadsheet. Then show him the numbered rows on the left side of the spreadsheet. Explain that these letters and numbers determine the cell name.

### 3. Practice

Call out a cell and have your child click in that cell. Make sure he clicked in the correct cell, and then call out a different cell.

## 4. Game

Play a game where your child types words into certain cells. For example, say, "type dog in cell D4" or "type cat in cell F11," and so on. Check your child's work as he goes, or check it after calling out several words. You may want to time your child and then play again and see if he can beat his previous time. Here is a list of words and cells that you could use.

| | | | |
|---|---|---|---|
| Dog | D4 | Cow | B3 |
| Cat | F11 | Horse | C8 |
| Mouse | G1 | Rabbit | E20 |
| Chicken | A10 | Snake | H15 |

## 5. Definitions

Instruct your child to write the definition of "spreadsheet" and "cell" into specific cells that you name. The definitions are given in the vocabulary section at the beginning of the chapter.

**Tip**
For extra practice, write down a list of 10 words with a specific cell name (letter and number) written next to them. Then have your child type the words into the correct cells on the spreadsheet.

Activity 6

# Spreadsheet Tutorials

## Goal

Your child will use an online tutorial to learn how to create a graph using a spreadsheet.

## Materials

- computer with Internet access
- paper and pencil
- spreadsheet program (Microsoft Excel or OpenOffice Calc)

## Steps

### 1. Prepare

Listed below are several online tutorials for creating graphs using Microsoft Excel and OpenOffice Calc. Choose the one that will be the best for your child's age and abilities. Become familiar with the website ahead of time, so you will know how to navigate the site. Your child could use more than one tutorial.

**Microsoft Excel Tutorials**

**evisa: Excel 2000:** www.evisa.com/e/sbooks/lib9/s58/slide01.htm

**Florida Gulf Coast University–Excel 2000 Tutorial: Charts:**
www.fgcu.edu/support/office2000/excel/charts.html

**Internet4Classrooms–Creating a Chart or Graph:**
www.internet4classrooms.com/excel_create_chart.htm

**Microsoft Office Online: Charts make data visual:**
http://office.microsoft.com/training/training.aspx?AssetID=RC10175736
1033&CTT=6&Origin=RP101757341033

**Microsoft Office Online Training Videos–Excel Charts and Graphs**
**Tutorial:** www.free-training-tutorial.com/charts-graphs.html

**OpenOffice Calc Tutorials**

**OpenOffice.org Calc In Pictures:** http://inpics.net/tutorials/calc2/vis9.html

**OpenOffice.org Calc Tutorial:** http://documentation.openoffice.org/tutorials/cospa/Cospa_Calc_Tutorial.pdf

**OpenOffice.org: Creating a Chart:** http://wiki.services.openoffice.org/wiki/Documentation/OOo3_User_Guides/Calc_Guide/Creating_a_chart

**Tutorials for OpenOffice: CALC:**
www.tutorialsforopenoffice.org/tutorial/Charting_Data.html

## 2. Tutorial

Allow your child to complete the online tutorials about graphs, or have her complete the sections that you want to focus on with her. You could have your child take notes from the site or complete any questions or quizzes that are included in the tutorial.

## 3. Share

Have your child share some interesting facts she has learned while viewing the tutorial.

**Tip**
You may want to have your child try a new skill when it is taught during the tutorial. After the tutorial, give her a few minutes to try some of the things she has learned.

Activity 7

# Graphing with a Spreadsheet

## Goal

Your child will gather data and then create a graph using a spreadsheet.

## Materials

- computer
- paper and pencil
- spreadsheet program (Microsoft Excel or OpenOffice Calc)
- printer
- paper for printer
- markers, crayons, or colored pencils (optional)

## Steps

### 1. Data

Allow your child to think of a question and then survey at least five people to find out their answers. Ask your child to think of a question such as "What is your favorite ice-cream flavor?" and then list a few possible answers: vanilla, chocolate, cookies and cream, or strawberry. Have your child record his results on paper and then use this information to create his graph.

Or, have your child gather data using other methods such as collecting online statistics, recording running times, reviewing prices, or any other method that he finds interesting. Allowing him to personally take part in the information gathering will allow him to see the relationship between statistics and the information on a graph.

## 2. Graph

Have your child follow these steps to create a graph in Microsoft Excel or OpenOffice Calc.

1. Open a new spreadsheet.

2. Insert data into cells.

3. Highlight the cells that you wish to appear on the graph.

4. Click on the Chart icon.

5. Complete the Chart Wizard.

## 3. Modify

Have your child double-click items (lines, bars, titles) on the graph to change the appearance (colors, styles, patterns).

## 4. Print

Show your child how to print the graph. Have your child explain the information that the graph illustrates.

## 5. Decorate

Provide markers, crayons, or colored pencils for your child to color the graph. You could display the graph in your home.

**Tips**

If needed, use the Help menu to search for a certain topic or use the spreadsheet tutorials from Activity 6 to learn more about how to use the spreadsheet.

For more practice creating graphs, allow your child to create several different types of graphs using the same data or create new data. Encourage your child to be creative when planning and designing his own graph.

Activity **8**

Easy to
Modify for
Younger Kids

# Formulas

## Goal

Your child will type a mathematical formula into a spreadsheet and then work out the problem using pencil and paper.

## Materials

- computer
- spreadsheet program (Microsoft Excel or OpenOffice Calc)
- pencil and paper

## Steps

### 1. Type

Have your child type four different formulas into a cell of the spreadsheet. Formulas begin with an = sign.

| Sign | Mathematical Operations | Sample Formulas |
| --- | --- | --- |
| * | Multiplication | =2*4 |
| + | Addition | =1+1 |
| − | Subtraction | =9–2 |
| / | Division | =4/2 |

### 2. Calculate

After your child types a formula into a cell, she should press Enter on the keyboard to calculate the results.

## 3. Check

Allow your child to check the answer by working the mathematical problem using pencil and paper.

**Tips**
If you need help showing your child how to type formulas, use the Help feature on your spreadsheet. For fun, try typing formulas that reference the numbers in other cells, such as "=A3*D2." Formulas can be complex, so if your child seems interested in learning more about formulas, use a tutorial to teach her more.

Activity 9

# Sorting

## Goal

Your child will type a list of words into a spreadsheet and then sort the list.

## Materials

- computer
- spreadsheet program (Microsoft Excel or OpenOffice Calc)

## Steps

### 1. Type

Have your child type a list of 10 words into cells A1 to A10 of a spreadsheet. He could type a list of names, colors, sports, countries, or anything else that interests him.

### 2. Highlight

Next, ask your child to highlight the cells A1 through A10.

### 3. Sort

Then have your child click the Sort Ascending icon (see icon at right) or select the Data menu tab and then click Sort > Ascending. This should put the list in alphabetical order.

### 4. Practice

Allow your child to sort descending and then ascending again.

> **Tip**
> For fun, give your child a list of words to put in alphabetical order and have him first write them on paper in alphabetical order. Then have him type the words into the spreadsheet and sort them ascending to check and make sure the words on the paper are all in the correct order.

Activity **10**

# Quiz

Easy to
Modify for
Younger Kids

## Goal

Your child will review graph and spreadsheet concepts and then take a quiz.

## Materials

- Graph and Spreadsheet Cards (CD Supplement 10F)
- Graphs and Spreadsheets Quiz I or II (CD Supplement 10G or 10H)
- Graphs and Spreadsheets Quiz I or II Answers (CD Supplement 10I or 10J)
- scissors
- computer
- spreadsheet program (Microsoft Excel or OpenOffice Calc)
- pencil

## Steps

### 1. Review

Use the Graph and Spreadsheet Cards (CD Supplement 10F) to review the terms. Print and cut apart the cards. Hold up each card and ask your child to tell you the definition of the term on the card. You could also have her use the computer to show you how to make the type of graph on the card. She could use the computer to show you a spreadsheet, cell, and even type in a formula.

### 2. Quiz

Decide which Graphs and Spreadsheets Quiz (I or II) will best meet the needs of your child, or she could take both quizzes. Print the appropriate quiz (CD Supplements 10G or 10H). Explain the instructions on the quiz. Give your child enough time to complete the quiz.

### 3. Check

Use the Graphs and Spreadsheets Quiz I or II Answers (CD Supplements 10I or 10J) to grade your child's work. Go over any missed questions with your child.

## Chapter 11

# Inside a Computer

## Objective

Children will be able to summarize knowledge of 18 computer parts by doing one or more of the following: drawing the part, explaining the purpose of the part, describing the part, examining the part, or locating the actual part.

## Purpose

Convey to your child the significance of knowing about computer parts. Your child will work harder to learn these terms if he knows it will help him in the future. Explain that it is important to know the name and function of basic computer parts to successfully operate computers. Explain that this chapter will broaden your child's understanding of how a computer works. Think of a unique way to provide reasons for learning so your child will be able to personally apply this information to his life. At the completion of this chapter, children should be able to recognize and explain the function of each computer part, enabling them to better understand computer processes.

## Activities Overview

This chapter will help your child understand computer parts and their functions through a variety of activities. The activities in this chapter will provide your child with the foundation and vocabulary needed to discuss and understand the rudiments of computers. The following chart categorizes each activity to help you to plan the lessons.

To get started, you may decide to plan a fun activity to inspire your child and focus your child's attention on technology. A lively event will prompt children to focus on the computer parts, and they will be more interested and ready to learn.

| Activities | Worksheet | Modifiable* | Internet Access | Game | Learning Cards | Slide Show | Arts and Crafts | Answer Key |
|---|---|---|---|---|---|---|---|---|
| 1. Computer Parts Slide Show | | ✔ | | | | ✔ | | |
| 2. Internet Research | ✔ | | ✔ | | | | | ✔ |
| 3. Identify the Computer Parts | | ✔ | | ✔ | | | | |
| 4. Make a Book | | ✔ | | | | | ✔ | |
| 5. Website Scavenger Hunt | | | ✔ | | | | | |
| 6. Computer Part Cards | ✔ | | | | ✔ | | | |
| 7. Matching Game | | ✔ | | ✔ | ✔ | | | |
| 8. Troubleshooting Computer Errors | | | | | | | | |
| 9. Cords and Cables | | | ✔ | | | | | |
| 10. Quiz | ✔ | | | | | | | ✔ |

* Easily modifiable for younger children

# CD Supplements

The following chart lists all of the CD supplements for this chapter and provides the CD filename, supplement title, and activity number. To make locating and using these supplements faster and easier, it is recommended that you copy all files to your hard drive before beginning the lessons.

| CD Filename | Title | Activity |
|---|---|---|
| 11A | Computer Parts Slide Show | 1,7 |
| 11B | Computer Parts Worksheet I | 2 |
| 11C | Computer Parts Worksheet II | 2 |
| 11D | Computer Parts Worksheet I Answers | 2 |
| 11E | Computer Parts Worksheet II Answers | 2 |
| 11F | Computer Part Cards | 6 |
| 11G | Computer Parts Quiz I | 10 |
| 11H | Computer Parts Quiz II | 10 |
| 11I | Computer Parts Quiz I Answers | 10 |
| 11J | Computer Parts Quiz II Answers | 10 |
| 11K | Build Your Own Computer Worksheet | Enrichment |
| 11L | Inside a Computer Vocabulary | Optional |

# Variations for Younger Children

Younger children learn differently and are motivated to explore concepts by different factors. Provide younger children with several opportunities to learn the computer parts, taking into account their various learning styles. Feel free to modify the activities, such as removing a step, to meet the needs of your child. This journey inside the computer should meet the needs of each child, which may mean guiding younger children at a much slower pace while responding to their interests and excitement along the way. Monitor your child's expression to see if she is showing signs of frustration because the activity is too difficult or signs of boredom because the activity is too easy then modify the activity to help her succeed on her individual level. You could even make up your own activities. The following ideas may help.

- Concentrate on fewer computer parts throughout the chapter. Use one website consistently when viewing the computer parts online.

- Have younger children participate in more hands-on experiences by encouraging them to examine the computer parts.

- You may not want to distribute fragile or expensive computer parts to younger children.

- Use a puppet to explain various computer parts.

- Encourage younger children to share facts learned while viewing the pictures and diagrams on the websites without completing the worksheet.

- Have younger children explain how the part works using their own words.

- Research a computer part together to show the technique for locating a part.

- Complete the quiz together with the younger child.

- Use the slide show presentation as an assessment. When your child sees the computer part, have her say the name of the part.

## Internet Safety

In this chapter, some activities require Internet access. Remind your child to think about Internet safety during these activities. You may want to review the Internet safety tips on pages 10–11.

## Fun Decorations

An inspiring room atmosphere and decorated walls will excite your children and focus their attention on technology. Decorations can generate enthusiasm as well as provide another opportunity to teach your children about computer parts. Be inventive as you plan the room decorations, and remember to have fun! The following are some ideas that might help you with decorations.

- Print each page of the Computer Parts Slide Show (CD Supplement 11A), glue the words and pictures to construction paper, and then hang them on a wall or door. It would work nicely to print six slides per page so you will be ready for Activity 7: Matching Game.

- Print out and glue several of the Computer Part Cards (CD Supplement 11F) to large shapes (circles, squares, triangles, etc.) cut from brightly colored construction paper, then hang the cards from the ceiling. You will also be able to use these cards for Activity 6: Computer Part Cards.

- Dedicate a section of your house to learning the computer parts. Refer to the information located in that area of your home throughout this chapter. Use a banner or letter cutouts to spell out "Inside a Computer," the topic of this chapter. Hang your child's completed work in this area.

- Change the screensaver or the desktop background of your computer to a picture of a computer part that your child will be learning about in this chapter.

- Hang some old computer parts from the ceiling with string.

## Vocabulary

Review the following terms with your child so that he or she can have a basic understanding of the vocabulary used in this chapter. You could also have your child write the definitions in the Inside a Computer Vocabulary worksheet (CD Supplement 11L).

**CD/DVD/Blu-ray drive:** The component that reads information from the CD (Compact Disc), DVD (Digital Video Disc), or Blu-ray disc.

**computer case:** It protects all of the electronic components inside and must have adequate ventilation to prevent overheating.

**CPU:** Central Processing Unit. The microprocessor. The "brains" of the computer.

**drive cables:** The cables that connect the drives to the motherboard.

**fan:** This is the primary source of cooling for your computer.

**floppy drive:** The component that reads and writes information to floppy disks.

**hard drive:** The component that reads and writes data to a hard disk. It stores information.

**memory card slot:** A slot that holds a small, portable memory card.

**modem:** This device transforms a computer's digital data into analog data for transmission over phone lines, then reconverts the data to digital.

**motherboard:** The main circuit board of your computer. This connects and enables the operation of all the components of the computer.

**network card:** A circuit board used to connect the computer to a local area network (LAN).

**PCI slot:** A slot on the motherboard used to add Peripheral Component Interconnect (PCI) expansion cards.

**ports:** Transmits information to and receives information from external devices.

**power supply:** The component that supplies power to your computer.

**RAM:** Random Access Memory. Data stored here can be deleted or created at any time. It is volatile.

**ROM:** Read-Only Memory. Data stored here cannot be deleted. It is nonvolatile.

**sound card:** A printed circuit board that, coupled with a set of speakers, enables a computer to reproduce music and sound effects.

**video card:** A printed circuit board that plugs into a personal computer to give it display capabilities.

# NETS•S Addressed

6. **Technology Operations and Concepts**

   Students demonstrate a sound understanding of technology concepts, systems, and operations. Students:

   a. understand and use technology systems

   b. select and use applications effectively and productively

c. troubleshoot systems and applications

d. transfer current knowledge to the learning of new technologies

## Grades

Think of the best way to determine your child's comprehension of the computer parts for each activity. This is your child's opportunity to demonstrate his individual understanding of the computer parts and their functions. Throughout each activity, evaluate your child while he works. When deciding on the type of assessment, consider his age and abilities. The following suggestions might help you to assess your child.

- Use the answer keys in the various activities to grade the supplements that your child completed. Base the grades on accuracy or completion. The answer keys can be found on the CD.

- You may want to use the Grade Book located in Appendix A at the back of this book to record your child's assignments and grades. Keep a running record of your child's progress to determine comprehension and understanding of the content. Record these observations on paper or in the Grade Book (Appendix A).

- Ask your child to write down the definitions to the vocabulary words in this chapter using the Inside a Computer Vocabulary worksheet (CD Supplement 11L).

- Observe your child as he researches, writes, locates the parts, shares information on computer parts, and documents his efforts.

- Have your child explain in his own words the purpose of certain computer parts.

- Direct your child to write down the importance of knowing the parts of a computer.

- Ask your child to display the appropriate way to handle fragile computer parts.

- Hold up a computer part and have your child write the name of the computer part on paper or type it using a word processor.

## Enrichment

Learning takes place all of the time, so motivate your child to learn more about the computer parts on her own. The excitement of learning about computer parts will probably motivate your child to learn more about technology. Children could become actively involved by deciding for themselves which enrichment activity to complete, causing them to really take ownership of the information. You could plan additional ways to expand your child's mind and her comprehension of computers. Be creative in thinking of an advanced assignment for high achievers. A variety of challenging and motivating ideas are offered in the following list.

- Use the Build Your Own Computer worksheet (CD Supplement 11K) as a guide to help your child design and possibly build a computer. Instruct your child to design her own computer and locate the prices of each part using the Internet.

- If you have a dial-up Internet connection, it may be interesting to your child if you play a recorded sound of a computer connecting to the Internet from a modem. Explain that this sound is heard when connecting to the Internet through a modem.

- Have your child research and then make a list of the various types of memory cards, such as CompactFlash, SmartMedia, Secure Digital Card (SD card), and MultiMediaCard (MMC) and explain how these cards work.

- Have your child find out the meaning of the different series of beeps that may come from the case speaker if something is wrong with your computer. These beeps are dependent on the type of motherboard that is in the computer. Computer Hope (www.computerhope.com/beep.htm) and 5 Star Support (www.5starsupport.com/info/beep_codes.htm) are two websites that list many samples of how the beep codes determine the computer error. Although no image is given on the monitor, the computer renders beep codes so you can determine where the error is on the computer.

- Take a field trip to a computer parts store (or any store with computers) and ask your child to write down all of the computer parts that she finds. Discuss the purposes of the parts.

- Instruct your child to draw a computer case and the parts inside, labeling each part.

- Direct your child to write a paper on the way that all the parts are connected and work together to make the computer system run properly.

- To motivate higher-level thinking, ask your child to suggest ways that computer parts may change in the future.

- Have your child research the history of a particular computer part and explain the various upgrades and changes made to the part over the years, such as the floppy drive.

- Encourage your child to design a computer part that will revolutionize the way computers work.

- Ask your child to find out why the floppy disk is called floppy.

## Closure

Give your child a a few minutes to reflect on all he has learned. This closing step is an important part of the learning process because the child has an opportunity to make the information his own. Choose one or more of the following ideas to complete this chapter.

- Have your child share navigation techniques that did and did not work when researching online. This could help children with future Internet research.

- Require your child to be accountable for knowing the computer parts and their functions in a few weeks. Think of an opportune time to ask your child about the computer parts a few weeks after you do the activities in this chapter. For example, as your child is working on the computer, you could ask him to tell you what he remembers about the parts inside a computer. Or maybe on a hot day when you have the fan or air conditioning running in your home, you could ask your child to name the computer part that keeps the computer cool. The answer is a case fan.

- Ask, "What have you learned concerning computer parts?" Encourage your child to share a few interesting facts or trivia that he has learned about computer parts.

- Ask your child to share any past computer experiences that he now understands better because of the information learned in this chapter.

Activity **1**

# Computer Parts Slide Show

Easy to
Modify for
Younger Kids

## Goal

Your child will recite the computer parts using a slide show presentation.

## Materials

* Computer Parts Slide Show (CD Supplement 11A)
* computer

## Steps

### 1. Prepare

Open the Computer Parts Slide Show (CD Supplement 11A).
Click Slide Show > View Slide Show when you are ready to begin.

### 2. Assess

Play the slide show, which shows a picture of the computer part then
the name of the part. As your child watches the slide show, have him
name any of the computer parts that he already knows. This is a great
way to assess child's knowledge of the computer parts in this chapter—
you may be surprised at how much your child already knows!

### 3. Recite

Play the slide show again and have your child recite the computer
parts as they appear on the screen. Tell your child to repeat after you if
he needs help saying the name of the part. Replay the slide show a few
times (if needed) to teach your child to correctly recite the names of
all these parts.

**Tip**
Add something new and interesting to the presentation such as
music, animation, or various slide backgrounds. To stimulate
higher-level thinking skills, during the slide show in Step 2 allow
your child to write down the name of the part and the function of
the part for any part that he already knows.

Activity 2

# Internet Research

## Goal

Your child will research the computer parts on a website, and then write the name of each computer part or the purpose of each part in the boxes provided on a worksheet.

## Materials

- Computer Parts Worksheet I or II (CD Supplement 11B or 11C)
- Computer Parts Worksheet I or II Answers (CD Supplement 11D or 11E)
- pencil
- computer with Internet access

## Steps

### 1. Prepare

Listed below are several websites that could be used to find the computer parts. Become familiar with the websites ahead of time so that you can decide which sites will best meet the abilities of your child.

**Click N Learn:** www.kids-online.net/learn/c_n_l.html

**How Stuff Works:** www.howstuffworks.com/pc.htm  —and—
    http://computer.howstuffworks.com/computer-peripherals-channel.htm
    **Note:** Use the How Stuff Works search engine

**Introduction to Computers:**
    www.grassrootsdesign.com/intro/hardware.php

**Jan's Illustrated Computer Literacy 101:**
    www.jegsworks.com/Lessons/lesson3/lesson3-1.htm

**Kids Domain Computer Connections: Computers Inside & Out:**
    www.kidsdomain.com/brain/computer/lesson/comp_les1.html

**TekMom's Technology Buzzwords for Children:**
    www.tekmom.com/buzzwords/#SearchBox

## 2. Teach

Show your child how to navigate the website and ways to locate the pictures and purposes of the computer parts. You may want to locate one of the terms together with your child.

## 3. Worksheets

Give your child either Computer Parts Worksheet I or II (CD Supplement 11B or 11C), depending on the abilities of your child.

In the Computer Parts Worksheet I (CD Supplement 11B), have your child use the websites to locate the 18 computer parts listed in the word list. Then have her write the name of the computer part next to the correct illustration.

You may need to help your child locate the computer parts. It may be fun to read some of the information on the sites while discussing the computer parts together. Strive to focus on the computer parts that seem to interest your child.

In the Computer Parts Worksheet II (CD Supplement 11C), allow your child to use the websites to discover the purpose of the 18 computer parts. Then ask her to write a description, using her own words, in the box provided.

Encourage your child to incorporate critical thinking skills when determining the purpose of each part. Your child should be excited to begin this Internet activity. Provide encouragement and support to help her discover information on her own.

## 4. Check

Use the Computer Parts Worksheet I or II Answers (CD Supplement 11D or 11E) to check your child's work. She could also use the answer key to self-check her work.

Easy to
Modify for
Younger Kids

Activity **3**

# Identify the Computer Parts

## Goal

Your child will locate and identify computer parts.

## Materials

* 18 computer parts (use as many as you have)

## Steps

### 1. Prepare

Place the computer parts on a table, or a specific location in a room. Use as many actual devices as possible to give children the opportunity to see the physical part. You could use a picture to represent the computer parts that you were unable to obtain for this activity.

For some parts, such as the ports and memory card slot, you could just point them out on your computer. If you feel comfortable doing so, you could take off the case covers and look inside your computer tower. I would not recommend opening a laptop because there is not much to see and the parts are delicate. Remember to turn off your computer and unplug it from the wall before opening the case. You could also take a field trip to a local computer repair store or a used computer parts store and ask if they have any old computer parts they could donate or allow you to see. You child will probably really enjoy this activity!

### 2. Locate

Ask, "Can you find the power supply?" Commend your child after he locates the power supply. If he is unable to locate the device on the table, give a hint to help him in locating it. For example: "This is the part that provides electricity to the computer."

## 3. Examine

Continue this exercise with the other computer parts. After locating the computer part, allow your child to look at it and examine it closely. Explain that computer parts are delicate and should be handled gently. Talk with your child about the different parts that he sees and discuss any interesting details.

## 4. Repeat

Repeat this activity asking more specific questions or the purpose of the part such as, "Can you find the part that allows your computer to play sound?" If your child is unable to locate the sound card on the table, give another hint to help find the card. For example, "Which circuit board has a place to plug in headphones?'

**Tips**

If you can obtain an old computer, you could take the computer apart with your child so that he will be able to conceptualize that all of the parts were in fact taken from the tower. Take a field trip to a local computer store and look at the various computer parts with your child.

This is a great hands-on activity for children who learn best by seeing and touching. Much of technology is virtual; however, in this activity your child will see and touch the actual objects.

Activity **4**

# Make a Book

Easy to Modify for Younger Kids

## Goal

Your child will make a book on computer parts.

## Materials

- markers or colored pencils
- white paper (any size or style)
- stapler
- construction paper (optional)
- stickers (optional)

## Steps

### 1. Draw

Ask your child to draw an illustration of one of the computer parts on a piece of blank paper while looking at the computer part or a picture of the part.

### 2. Label

Have your child write the name of the part on the paper. Allow her to be creative and write it anywhere on the paper.

### 3. Purpose

Instruct your child to write the purpose of the part, describing what it does. Repeat steps 1–3 for each part.

## 4. Decorate

Allow your child to decorate each page using markers, colored pencils, or stickers. Your child could make a cover for the book from construction paper. Have your child staple the pages together to make a book.

## 5. Read

Allow your child to read the book to you or someone else.

**Tip**
Allow your child to cut out pictures of these computer parts from old magazines or catalogs and glue them to the specific page of that term in her book. Instruct your child to locate certain facts about an assigned computer part, such as the purpose, size, placement, dependence on other parts, and various styles, and then write that information on the corresponding page.

Activity 5

# Website Scavenger Hunt

## Goal

Your child will search for certain computer parts, pictures, or facts on websites.

## Materials

- computer with Internet Access
- paper and pencil

## Steps

### 1. Prepare

Choose a website and make a list of certain computer parts, pictures, or facts that you would like your child to find on that site. You could use some computer parts that your child needs to practice or choose new computer parts that you would like to teach.

**Click N Learn:** www.kids-online.net/learn/c_n_l.html

**How Stuff Works:** www.howstuffworks.com/pc.htm  *–and–*
   http://computer.howstuffworks.com/computer-peripherals-channel.htm
   **Note:** Use the How Stuff Works search engine

**Introduction to Computers:**
   www.grassrootsdesign.com/intro/hardware.php

**Jan's Illustrated Computer Literacy 101:**
   www.jegsworks.com/Lessons/lesson3/lesson3-1.htm

**Kids Domain Computer Connections: Computers Inside & Out:**
   www.kidsdomain.com/brain/computer/lesson/comp_les1.html

**TekMom's Technology Buzzwords for Children:**
   www.tekmom.com/buzzwords/#SearchBox

## 2. Directions

Explain to your child that he should look on the website for a particular word, such as "modem;" or a picture, such as a picture of a network card; or a certain fact, such as the purpose of a CD/DVD drive. Depending on the age of your child, you may need to help him navigate the site.

## 3. Begin

Have your child open the site and begin searching for the items on your list. You could have him make a check mark next to the item on the paper when it is located on the site.

**Tip**
Time your child for each item to find out which items were the quickest to locate and which ones were more difficult. Create a fill-in-the-blank worksheet for your child by writing a sentence from a website leaving one word out. Your child must search for the missing word.

Activity 6

# Computer Part Cards

## Goal

Your child will identify computer parts by labeling them with the computer part cards.

## Materials

- Computer Part Cards (CD Supplement 11F)
- scissors
- tape
- 18 computer parts (use as many as you have)

## Steps

### 1. Prepare

Print the Computer Part Cards (CD Supplement 11F) from the CD and then cut them apart. Or you may decide to write the names of the computer parts on index cards using a marker.

### 2. Discuss

Show each card to your child give her an opportunity to tell you about the part and explain the purpose of the part to you. If your child is still learning to read, just read the card for her, and then allow her to share. You could also describe the function of a particular part, and then your child could find the corresponding card.

### 3. Label

Have your child label the computer parts in your room by taping the word cards to them. If you don't have some of the computer parts, just allow your child to explain what it looks like or what it does.

## 4. Check

Check each card to see if your child put the card in the correct place. If your child needs extra practice, do the activity again.

**Tip**
Try to have your child memorize the various names of the computer parts. If you show your enthusiasm and interest while teaching, your child will catch the excitement to learn. Think of a fun way to instruct your child and motivate her by actively involving her in this activity. Hold up one of the Computer Part Cards (CD Supplement 11F), and have her write the purpose of the part on a piece of paper.

Easy to
Modify for
Younger Kids

Activity 7

# Matching Game

## Goal

Your child will play a game by matching a word card with a picture of the computer part.

## Materials

- Computer Parts Slide Show (CD Supplement 11A)
- printer
- paper for printer
- construction paper (optional)

## Steps

### 1. Prepare

Print the slides from the Computer Parts Slide Show (CD Supplement 11A) and cut them out. When printing, you should print several slides per page. It would work nicely to print six slides per page. You may need to glue or tape the slides to construction paper so you cannot see through the paper for the game.

### 2. Review

Before you begin, you may want to review the picture of each part and the name of the part with your child.

### 3. Position Cards

Place all of the cards upside down on the floor or table to play the matching game. You could choose only a few of the cards and their matches and play a shorter version first.

## 4. *Play*

Your child will pick up one card and then pick up another card and try to find the corresponding card. For example, to get a match, your child will need a card that says "fan" and the card with a picture of a fan. When your child gets a match, he keeps it. Continue until your child has matched all of the cards with the corresponding card. Then, mix up all of the cards and play again.

**Tip**
You could play this game with your child, and another sibling or friend could play as well. After all of the matches are made, the player with the most matches at the end of the game wins. To make the game easier, just use a few of the cards and their matches.

Activity 8

# Troubleshooting Computer Errors

## Goal

Your child will think about how to fix common computer errors.

## Materials

- computer or paper and pencil

## Steps

### 1. Prepare

Ask your child to think about some common errors or possible problems that could occur with your computer using some of the parts in this chapter. You could make a list with your child using paper and pencil or type it using a word processor.

### 2. Discuss

Talk with your child about some common errors that could occur with your computer and plan a way to fix the problem. Here are a few examples (Complex system interdependencies have not been taken into consideration):

- If a computer is not able to connect to the Internet, the modem or network card may need to be checked because these parts allow Internet connectivity.

- If the CD/DVD drive is not reading the discs, it may need to be replaced because the CD/DVD drive reads information from the discs.

- If the computer does not turn on, the power supply may need to be replaced because it supplies power to the computer system.

## 3. Troubleshooting

Plan a way to incorporate some of your child's ideas when trouble-shooting your computer system. You may want to tell your child that you are going to cause an error and she will need to tell you how to fix the problem. For example, you could unplug your wireless Internet card or your Ethernet or phone cable that allows your computer to connect to the Internet. Then, when your child determines that the computer cannot connect to the Internet, help her determine how to fix the problem. Your child will feel proud to have helped you fix a computer problem.

Activity **9**

# Cords and Cables

## Goal

Your child will learn that all the cords and parts work together to make the computer function properly.

## Materials

- several cords and their corresponding computer parts

## Steps

### 1. Prepare

Place the cords and parts on a table.

### 2. Match Cords to Parts

Ask your child to match the cord or cable with the corresponding computer part (see sample below).

telephone cord ......................... modem

network cable ......................... network card

drive cable .............................. hard drive, CD/DVD drive, motherboard

power cable ............................ power supply

### 3. Explain

Have your child explain the reason that these parts go together.

> **Tip**
> Explain that each part has a purpose and a reason for its position in the computer system. It takes all of the parts to work in an organized fashion to make the computer function properly.

Activity **10**

# *Quiz*

## Goal

Your child will take a computer parts quiz.

## Materials

- Computer Parts Quiz I or II (CD Supplements 11G or 11H)
- Computer Parts Quiz I or II Answers (CD Supplements 11I or 11J)
- computer or pencil

## Steps

### *1. Prepare*

Decide which Computer Parts Quiz (I or II) will best meet the needs of your child. Print the appropriate quiz (CD Supplement 11G or 11H).

### *2. Quiz*

Explain the instructions at the top of the assessment. Give your child enough time to take the quiz to determine all that she has learned about computer parts during this chapter. Go over any questions.

### *3. Check*

Use the Computer Parts Quiz I or II Answers (CD Supplement 11I or 11J) to grade your child's work. Go over any missed questions with your child.

**Tip**
It might be fun and challenging to have your child take the Computer Parts Quiz II (CD Supplement 11H.doc) using the computer. Your child could type in the capital letters in the boxes.

## Chapter 12

# Web 2.0 Activities

## Objective

Children will experience and learn the basics of several Web 2.0 concepts including blogs, podcasts, RSS (Really Simple Syndication) feeds, wikis, and video-sharing sites while practicing Internet safety.

## Purpose

Using the Internet to stay connected with family and friends has become more popular, and this chapter teaches children some of the basic concepts surrounding this fairly new type of online communication. A variety of activities are used to show children how to use blogs, podcasts, RSS feeds, wikis, and video-sharing sites as well as how to stay safe when communicating online. Make this chapter meaningful by explaining the importance of knowing how to communicate using the Internet appropriately and ethically.

# Activities Overview

The activities in this chapter offer a solid foundation for communicating online socially. At the completion of this chapter, your child should have a sound understanding of blogs, podcasts, RSS feeds, wikis, and video-sharing sites. The following chart categorizes each activity to help you to plan the lessons.

To get started, you may decide to plan a fun activity to inspire your child and focus your child's attention on online social communication. You could show your child any online social communication sites that you use and how it helps you to stay in contact with your friends and family. You may even have a story to share about how you keep your personal information safe from potentially dangerous people. A lively event will prompt children to focus on communicating using the Internet, and they will be more interested and ready to learn.

| Activities | Worksheet | Modifiable* | Internet Access | Game | Learning Cards | Slide Show | Arts and Crafts | Answer Key |
|---|---|---|---|---|---|---|---|---|
| 1. Blog Slide Show | | ✔ | | | | ✔ | ✔ | |
| 2. Blogging | | | ✔ | | | | | |
| 3. Blog Quiz | ✔ | | | | | | | ✔ |
| 4. Podcast Slide Show | | ✔ | | | | ✔ | ✔ | |
| 5. RSS Feeds | | | ✔ | | | | | |
| 6. Podcasting | | | ✔ | | | | | |
| 7. Podcast Quiz | ✔ | | | | | | | ✔ |
| 8. Wiki | | | ✔ | | | | | |
| 9. Video-Sharing Sites | | ✔ | ✔ | | | | | |
| 10. Make a Book | | ✔ | | | | | ✔ | |

* Easily modifiable for younger children

# CD Supplements

The following chart lists all of the CD supplements for this chapter and provides the CD filename, supplement title, and activity number. To make locating and using these supplements faster and easier, it is recommended that you copy all files to your hard drive before beginning the lessons.

| CD Filename | Title | Activity |
|---|---|---|
| 12A | Blog Slide Show | 1 |
| 12B | Blog Quiz I | 3 |
| 12C | Blog Quiz II | 3 |
| 12D | Blog Quiz I Answers | 3 |
| 12E | Blog Quiz II Answers | 3 |
| 12F | Podcast Slide Show | 4 |
| 12G | Podcast Quiz I | 7 |
| 12H | Podcast Quiz II | 7 |
| 12I | Podcast Quiz I Answers | 7 |
| 12J | Podcast Quiz II Answers | 7 |
| 12K | Web 2.0 Activities Vocabulary | Optional |

# Variations for Younger Children

Children are exposed to the computer at an early age and should learn how to communicate appropriately when using the Internet. Prepare appropriate activities that will allow your child to explore ideas while giving him sufficient exposure to the online social communication concepts. Feel free to modify the activities, such as removing a step, to meet the needs of your child. Monitor your child's expression to see if he is showing signs of frustration because the activity is too difficult or signs of boredom because the activity is too easy then modify the activity to help him succeed on his individual level. You could even make up your own activities. The following ideas may help.

- Create a booklet by printing some of the slides from the slide shows (CD Supplement 12A and 12F) so that your child can read about blog and podcast concepts and look at the pictures on his own. He could color this booklet for added fun! You could also have him look at this booklet during the slide shows.

- Concentrate on a few of the vocabulary terms, instead of all of the terms that are discussed throughout the chapter. You may want to expose your child to all of the terms, but focus on one or two terms at a time.

- Use a central theme for all of the activities based on something that your child is currently learning about, such as nursery rhymes, holidays, food, families, or the solar system. This will allow your child to work with familiar concepts while learning about blogs, podcasts, wikis, and video-sharing sites.

## Internet Safety

In this chapter, some activities require Internet access. Remind your child to think about Internet safety during these activities. You may want to review the Internet safety tips on pages 10–11.

In some of the activities in this Web 2.0 chapter, your child may be given the opportunity to design and upload information to the Internet. If you allow your child to upload her work to the Internet, remind her about the importance of being safe when going online. It may be difficult for children to understand the ramifications of posting certain information, especially if the events may happen in the future. Children need to understand that the information they publish online may be available for anyone to see, read, and print and could provide a way to find out personal information about them. Explain to your child at an early age why she might not want a certain picture floating around the Internet or a certain personal story shared with the world now and even when she is grown. Make sure your child understands that once you publish something on the Internet it will always be available and is difficult to delete; therefore, she should not write and publish anything on the Internet that she wants to keep private.

Closely monitor and allow your child to publish only those things you feel are appropriate for everyone to see. Stress the importance of you reviewing the information that she wants to upload before she publishes it, for her protection and privacy both now and in the future. Encourage your child to use general topics and information, such as puzzles, jokes, math problems, stories, favorite hobbies, clothing design, recipes, or other topics that do not reveal anything about her. You may want to consider posting the information to a private server with firewall protection in your home instead of the web, giving your child the opportunity to see her work published in a safe environment.

## Fun Decorations

Do something different at your house for this chapter by creating an environment that will excite your child about Web 2.0 activities. Decorations can generate enthusiasm as well as provide another opportunity to teach your child about blogs, podcasts, wikis, and video-sharing websites. Be inventive as you plan the room decorations, and remember to have fun! The following are some ideas that might help you with decorations.

- Print some of the pages from the slide shows in this chapter, the Blog Slide Show (CD Supplement 12A) or the Podcast Slide Show (CD Supplement 12F). Glue them to construction paper and then hang them on a wall or door.

- Dedicate a section of your house to learning about Web 2.0. Refer to the information located in that area of your home throughout this chapter. Use a banner or letter cutouts to spell out "Web 2.0 Activities." the topic of this chapter. Hang completed work in this area.

- Change the screensaver or the desktop background of your computer to a picture, such as an iPod or a podcast icon, that represents something that your child will be learning about in this chapter.

- Display a globe or a picture of the Earth to refer to throughout the chapter to create visual images reminding your child that the Internet spans the entire world.

- Select a theme for this chapter, such as music, animals, or sports. Decorate the room with creative items based on the theme. Change the desktop background on the computer to a picture of the chosen theme. During the activities, have your child create his blog, podcast, and wiki based on this theme.

- Use a large poster board to create a pretend blog on the wall based on your child's favorite sports teams (or another topic). You could title the board "Our Family Blog." Throughout the chapter allow your family to share information about their favorite sports team by writing on this board. This is a great way for your child to see that blogs represent real information. The information on this board could be used in Activity 2: Blogging.

# Vocabulary

Review the following terms with your child so that he or she can have a basic understanding of the vocabulary used in this chapter. You could also have your child write the definitions in the Web 2.0 Activities Vocabulary worksheet (CD Supplement 12K).

**blog:** A website with a personal journal that is usually updated regularly. (Short for "Web log.")

**blogger:** A person who writes a blog.

**blogging:** Writing in a blog.

**blogosphere:** The collection of all blogs on the Internet.

**broadcasting:** Distributing audio files via streaming technologies.

**iPod:** A personal digital media player created by Apple.

**podcast:** Audio and video files that are downloaded from a website to be played on a computer or a mobile device. (Term comes from "iPod" and "broadcasting")

**podcast icon:** Podcasts are identified by a podcast icon on the Internet.

**podcaster:** A person who creates a podcast.

**podcasting:** The process of making audio or video podcasts available via the Internet.

**RSS (Really Simple Syndication) feeds:** A file written in XML that can be read on your computer, allowing you to read news or webpage snippets within a simple console.

**social networking site:** A website where users create personal profiles and communicate with others online. For example, Facebook, MySpace, Xanga

**subscribe:** Sign up to automatically receive podcasts when new episodes are posted.

**Web 2.0:** A term used to describe the way the World Wide Web is used as a social network, where people can easily communicate and work together online using tools such as blogs, podcasts, wikis, and video-sharing sites.

**wiki:** A website that allows users to quickly update and add information.

**video-sharing site:** A website where you can view, upload, and share video clips.

# NETS•S Addressed

2. **Communication and Collaboration**

Students use digital media and environments to communicate and work collaboratively, including at a distance, to support individual learning and contribute to the learning of others. Students:

   a. interact, collaborate, and publish with peers, experts, or others employing a variety of digital environments and media

   b. communicate information and ideas effectively to multiple audiences using a variety of media and formats

   c. develop cultural understanding and global awareness by engaging with learners of other cultures

   d. contribute to project teams to produce original works or solve problems

5. **Digital Citizenship**

Students understand human, cultural, and societal issues related to technology and practice legal and ethical behavior. Students:

   a. advocate and practice the safe, legal, and responsible use of information and technology

   b. exhibit a positive attitude toward using technology that supports collaboration, learning, and productivity

   c. demonstrate personal responsibility for lifelong learning

   d. exhibit leadership for digital citizenship

# Grades

Determine a way to authentically evaluate your child based on his individual accomplishments and creative abilities. Throughout each activity, evaluate your child while he works. When deciding on the type of assessment, consider his age and abilities and give clear expectations so that he understands all that is expected of him and as a result he can be successful. The following are some suggestions that might help you to assess your child.

- Use the answer keys in the various activities to grade the supplements that your child completed. Base the grades on accuracy or completion. The answer keys can be found on the CD.

- You may want to use the Grade Book located in Appendix A at the back of this book to record your child's assignments and grades. Keep a running record of your child's progress to determine comprehension and understanding of the content. Record these observations on paper or in the Grade Book (Appendix A).

- Ask your child to write down the definitions to the vocabulary words in this chapter using the Web 2.0 Activities Vocabulary worksheet (CD Supplement 12K).

- Observe and document the efforts of your child while he is watching slide shows and taking notes.

- Have your child tell you why it is important to always behave ethically, especially when communicating online.

- Have your child print his blog, wiki, and any other work that he created so that you can see his work. This will also give your child the ability to see his work in a printed format, reminding him that it is permanent. Remind him that once you upload or publish something, anyone can print it out and show it to anyone.

# Enrichment

The information learned in this chapter, including blogs, podcasts, RSS feeds, wikis, video-sharing sites, and social networking, may have motivated your child to want to learn more Web 2.0 concepts. Think of additional ways to challenge your child and expand her knowledge. A variety of challenging and motivating ideas are offered in the following list.

- Encourage your child to complete an online tutorial on any of the concepts learned in this chapter to learn more.

- Ask your child to research Web 2.0 and explain how the Internet has recently changed to contain more social networking websites.

- Have your child keep a journal for one week that could be a pretend blog.

- Instruct your child to research the dangers of blogging using personal information and to share the information she has learned with your family.

- Make a podcast to use with your child. Have your child subscribe to the podcast to get your new podcasts automatically.

- Record stories, poems, and songs for your child to listen to while she is playing. Your child could record them, too.

- Go to the store and look at iPods or other digital media devices. This would be a great opportunity for your child to see different digital media devices.

- Encourage your child to use various recording equipment (if available) to create her podcast.

- Have your child research to find the most popular social networking site and explain why she thinks it is so popular.

- Ask your child to research how RSS feeds work and write a paragraph describing this process.

- Have your child design and create a video regarding the importance of being safe when communicating online.

- Have your child think about and write a report discussing how video-sharing sites are fun, but also a place to be cautious when searching and watching videos online.

## Closure

Promote a sense of accomplishment and allow a few moments for your child to think about all he has created and learned in this chapter. This allows your child to process and reflect upon all that he has learned about the Web 2.0 concepts. The following are some suggestions for closure activities.

- Encourage your child to share a few interesting facts or trivia that he has learned during this chapter. Ask, "What have you learned about blogs, podcasts, RSS feeds, wikis, and video-sharing sites?"

- Ask your child to share a story or personal experience concerning the concepts learned about the right and wrong way to communicate online.

- Hold a celebration of a job well done and praise your child, who has worked hard to create his blog, podcast, and wiki. Present an award to your child for his accomplishments.

Activity **1**

# Blog Slide Show

Easy to
Modify for
Younger Kids

## Goal

Your child will watch a slide show to learn some introductory information and terms regarding blogs.

## Materials

- Blog Slide Show (CD Supplement 12A)
- computer
- paper and pencil
- markers, crayons, or colored pencils

## Steps

### 1. Prepare

Open the Blog Slide Show (CD Supplement 12A).
Click Slide Show > View Slide Show when you are ready to begin.

### 2. Learn

As you advance each slide, have your child read along with you to learn about the following concepts: the definition of blog, blogger, blogging, and blogosphere; blog facts; types of blogs; and possible topics of blogs. Ask your child to tell you about any of the blogging terms that he already knows while watching the slide show. The slide show also includes some Internet safety concepts that are discussed more in Chapter 2: "Safety on the Internet."

### 3. Review

Show the slide show again and ask your child recall the meanings of the terms before they appear on the screen. Your child could advance the slides during the multimedia presentation. You may want to instruct your child to take notes and write down the terms and definitions from the slide show.

## 4. Draw

Have your child choose one term from the slide show to illustrate on paper. Ask him to write the term and the definition and then draw a picture that represents the term. Allow him to decorate his paper with markers, crayons, or colored pencils.

**Tip**
Explain that a blog is like a journal that is posted online for everyone to read.

Activity **2**

# Blogging

## Goal

Your child will view a blog online and then design a blog.

## Materials

- computer with Internet access
- word processor (Microsoft Word or OpenOffice Writer)
- printer and paper

## Steps

### 1. View

Locate one or more blogs online that would be of interest to your child, such as blogs covering local community events, political elections, or sports events, and show it to your child so she knows what an actual blog looks like. While viewing the blog, point out some of the characteristics that make it a blog website, such as the date, pictures, links, archived files, and posts.

### 2. Design

Have your child use the word processing skills she learned in Chapter 5: "Word Processing" to create and type a blog. Think of a fun way to guide your child as she creates her own blog. Explain that blogs are a place to share ideas and opinions, not private or personal information. Your child can get as creative as she likes with this activity by including pictures, dates, surveys, and other items typically found on a blog. Make up a fun topic or allow your child to come up with her own topic and design. Your child could pick a topic that she finds interesting from the following list.

- Write a review about a children's book, poem, verse, or other printed material.
- Gather data using a variety of methods such as surveying, collecting online statistics, or conducting an opinion poll. Record the data on paper to be used on the blog.
- Make up a news report on a local event, the weather, or upcoming events.

- Discuss opinions on politics or environmental issues.
- Write a story.
- Make up a recipe or even a cookbook.
- Describe how to stay in shape by sharing some fun exercise routines.
- Design a card game and give instructions on how to play it.

## 3. Review

Read over your child's blog and check for grammatical errors. Have your child review it as well and make any necessary changes.

## 4. Print

Have your child print out her blog. Seeing her blog in printed form will remind her that the information on blogs can be printed and shared with others.

## 5. Upload

If you want to allow your child to upload the blog to an actual website, here are a few links that may help you. Review your child's information carefully and discuss with your child the ramifications of posting personal information online, because once it is uploaded, anyone can read it, and it is very difficult to delete.

**About.com–Tutorial: How to Start a Free Blog at Blogger.com:**
http://weblogs.about.com/od/creatingablog/ss/BloggerTutorial.htm

**About.com–How To Create a Blog for Free in 4 Easy Steps:**
http://weblogs.about.com/od/creatingablog/ht/CreateBlog5Step.htm

**Education World: Build a Blog Portal:**
www.educationworld.com/a_tech/techtorial/techtorial100.pdf

**GCFLearnFree.org–Create Your Own Blog: It's As Easy as 1, 2, 3!:**
www.gcflearnfree.org/computer/article.aspx?tid=15&aid=179

**Tip**
Encourage your child to share examples of how blogs can be helpful to her personally or to the community.

Activity **3**

# *Blog Quiz*

## Goal

Your child will take a quiz on blogs.

## Materials

- Blog Quiz I or II (CD Supplement 12B or 12C)
- Blog Quiz I or II Answers (CD Supplement 12D or 12E)
- pencil

## Steps

### 1. *Prepare*

Decide which Blog Quiz (I or II) will be the best way to assess your child. Print the appropriate quiz (CD Supplement 12B or 12C).

### 2. *Quiz*

Explain the instructions at the top of the assessment. Go over any questions. Give your child enough time to take the quiz to determine all that he has learned about blogs.

### 3. *Check*

Use the Blog Quiz I or II Answers (CD Supplement 12D or12E) to grade your child's work. Go over any missed questions with your child.

Activity **4**

# Podcast Slide Show

## Goal

Your child will watch a slide show to learn about podcasts and then illustrate a vocabulary term.

## Materials

- Podcast Slide Show (CD Supplement 12F)
- computer
- paper and pencil
- markers, crayons, or colored pencils

## Steps

### 1. Prepare

Open the Podcast Slide Show (CD Supplement 12F).
Click Slide Show > View Slide Show when you are ready to begin.

### 2. Learn

As you advance each slide, have your child read along with you to learn about the following concepts: the definition of podcast, iPod, broadcasting, podcaster, podcasting, and RSS feeds, as well as other facts about podcasts. Your child could tell you about any of the podcast terms that she already knows while watching the slide show. The slide show also includes some Internet safety concepts that are discussed more in Chapter 2: "Safety on the Internet."

### 3. Review

Show the slide show again and have your child recall the meanings of the terms before they appear on the screen. Your child could advance the slides during the multimedia presentation. If desired, instruct your child to take notes and write down the terms and definitions from the slide show.

## 4. *Draw*

Have your child choose one concept from the slide show to illustrate on paper. Ask her to write the term and the definition and then draw a picture that represents the concept. Allow her to decorate her paper with markers, crayons, or colored pencils.

> **Tip**
> You can listen to podcasts at any time. It might be fun for your child to listen to podcasts when she is playing or maybe on a long car ride, if you have a portable media device.

Activity **5**

# RSS Feeds

## Goal

Your child will listen to podcasts, subscribe to podcasts using RSS feeds, and then find and listen to downloaded podcasts.

## Materials

* computer with Internet access
* paper and pencil

## Steps

### 1. Prepare

Before this activity, locate a few websites with podcasts that your child will find interesting. You could choose podcasts that may be of interest to your child, such as his favorite book or extracurricular activity, or even something that you want him to memorize. Be sure to preview the podcast to make sure it is suitable for your child and does not include any obscene language or inappropriate content. Here are a few websites where you can find podcasts especially for kids.

> **iTunes:** www.itunes.com
>
> **Kid-Cast.com:** www.kid-cast.com (available through iTunes)
>
> **LearnOutLoud.com:** www.learnoutloud.com/contents/
> All-LearnOutLoud.coms-Podcasts/9/21
>
> **The Education Podcast Network:** www.epnweb.org

### 2. Listen

Allow your child to listen to a few different audio podcasts or view video podcasts using the computer. Have your child point out the ones he likes, the ones he does not like, and why. This may help your child to choose the type of podcast he would like to create for the next activity. Have your child write down a possible topic and some things he would like to discuss during his podcast.

## 3. Subscribe

Show your child how to subscribe to an RSS feed that he is interested in so that he can sign up to automatically receive podcasts when new episodes are posted. If you need help subscribing to the RSS feeds, use one of the following sites.

**Education World: Understanding RSS Feeds:**
www.educationworld.com/a_tech/techtorial/techtorial103.pdf

**How Stuff Works: How RSS Works:**
http://computer.howstuffworks.com/rss.htm/printable

**RSS: A Quick Start Guide for Educators:**
http://static.hcrhs.k12.nj.us/gems/tech/RSSFAQ4.pdf

## 4. View

When a new podcast is automatically downloaded, show your child how to find and listen to the podcast.

**Tip**
Podcasts are different from other files because you can subscribe to podcasts that you want to be downloaded automatically. When you subscribe to a podcast, if new podcasts are posted online, the files are automatically downloaded to a specific location on your computer.

Activity 6

# *Podcasting*

## Goal

Your child will design and record a podcast.

## Materials

- computer with Internet access
- audio-editing software
- RSS reader
- paper and pencil
- microphone
- headphones
- video camera (if creating a video podcast)
- various children's books, poems, rhymes (optional)

## Steps

### 1. Prepare

Before this activity, locate and practice using the audio and video software and equipment available on your computer so that you will be able to instruct your child on how to use them. You could write down the steps for your child to follow and even include pictures next to the steps when explaining how to use your recording equipment.

Examples of audio-editing software that may be available on your computer are Sound Recorder (Windows) or GarageBand (Mac). Another good choice for audio-editing software is Audacity, a free cross-platform program available for download at http://audacity. sourceforge.net. If you do not have a microphone or a video camera, maybe you could borrow one from a friend or the local library.

If you need more information on creating a podcast, or converting and uploading the file to an actual website, here are a few links that may help you.

**Education World—Creating a Podcast:**
www.educationworld.com/a_tech/techtorial/techtorial092.pdf

**Guides and Tutorials.com: Introduction to Podcasting:**
www.guidesandtutorials.com/podcasting-tutorial.html

**How to Podcast:** www.how-to-podcast-tutorial.com

## 2. Design

Make up a fun topic, have your child come up with her own topic, or allow your child to pick a topic that she finds interesting from the following list to design her own podcast. Next, she should write down some notes, an outline, or exactly what she wants to say during her podcast. Encourage your child to be creative when planning and designing her own podcast.

- Have your child record herself reading a children's book, poem, verse, or other printed material. If your child reads a book, she could ring a bell or play a certain sound when it is time to turn the page. Your child may tell a nursery rhyme, such as "Humpty Dumpty," tell a story such as Pocahontas, or read a book such as *Cinderella* for her recording.

- Allow your child to gather data using a variety of methods—surveying, collecting online statistics, conducting an opinion poll, or any other method the your child finds interesting. Instruct your child to record her data on paper to be used to create the podcast.

- Have your child say the alphabet in a different language. This might be a great way to memorize words in a different language because children learn quickly through repetition.

- Ask her to make up a news report on a local event, the weather, or upcoming events.

- Have your child sing a song such as "Itsy Bitsy Spider," her favorite song, or even a song that she has written herself. She could even use musical instruments such as a guitar or violin.

## 3. Record

Have your child independently create a unique podcast. Show your child how to use the audio or video recording equipment and software then allow her to practice until she feels comfortable. Let your child know how you are going to grade her work by explaining any criteria you would like her to include in the podcasts. Encourage your child to do her best work when she is recording.

## 4. Play

Allow your child to play her recording for a friend or another family member. You can play it using a computer or a portable media device such as an iPod.

## 5. Upload

If your child will be uploading her podcast to the Internet, carefully review her recording. Remember to be careful when uploading anything to the Internet to keep your child safe. Never allow your child to upload any personal information. Remind your child that once you upload anything to the Internet, it is difficult to remove it.

Remember to consider copyright laws if your child reads a story or writes a story based on a previously published work. Listed below are a couple informative websites on copyright laws.

**United States Copyright Office:** www.copyright.gov

**10 Big Myths about copyright explained:**
www.templetons.com/brad/copymyths.html

**Tip**
Demonstrate for your child how to use the recording equipment correctly, such as not tapping on the microphone. Discuss the importance of taking care of the computer and the recording equipment to keep it working properly.

Activity **7**

# *Podcast Quiz*

## Goal

Your child will take a quiz on podcasts.

## Materials

- Podcast Quiz I or II (CD Supplement 12G or 12H)
- Podcast Quiz I or II Answers (CD Supplement 12I or 12J)
- pencil

## Steps

### 1. *Prepare*

Decide which Podcast Quiz (I or II) will best meet the needs of your child. Print the appropriate quiz (CD Supplement 12G or 12H).

### 2. *Quiz*

Explain the instructions at the top of the quiz. Go over any questions. Give your child enough time to take the quiz to determine all that he has learned about podcasts.

### 3. *Check*

Use the Podcast Quiz I or II Answers (CD Supplement 12I or 12J) to grade your child's work. Go over any missed questions with your child.

**Tip**
For something different, open the quiz on the computer screen and allow your child to take the quiz using the computer. He could underline and change the font color to show his answers.

Activity **8**

# *Wiki*

## Goal

Your child will design and then create a wiki.

## Materials

- computer with Internet access
- paper and pencil

## Steps

### 1. Prepare

Wikis are websites that allow users to easily update and add information. Here are a couple websites that can help you teach your child about wikis.

> **Working with Wikis:**
> www.educationworld.com/a_tech/techtorial/techtorial098.shtml

> **How Wikis Work:** http://computer.howstuffworks.com/wiki.htm

You can also refer to the sites listed in Step 5: Upload if you are planning to allow your child to create a wiki on the Internet.

### 2. View

View a few popular wikis with your child such as www.wikipedia.com *or* www.wikihow.com so she can get some ideas for her own wiki.

### 3. Topic

Make up a fun topic, have your child come up with her own topic, or allow your child to pick a topic that she finds interesting from the following list.

- an encyclopedia wiki about the oceans of the world or another science topic

- a vocabulary list of the terms in this chapter
- a wiki about the life of a favorite president or historical figure
- a review of a television show or book
- a wiki filled with puzzles and surveys
- a learning tutorial that teaches mathematical concepts

## 4. Design

Have your child write down some notes and show a layout of her wiki. Let your child know how you are going to grade her work by explaining any criteria you would like her to include in her wiki.

## 5. Upload

Consider whether or not you are going to allow your child to create a wiki on the Internet. Remember to be careful when creating anything that will appear on the Internet to keep your child safe. Never allow her to include any personal information. Remind your child that once you upload anything to the Internet it is difficult to remove it. The following is a list of sites that host wiki webpages that you might want to use if you are publishing your child's work.

**Pbworks:** http://pbworks.com

**Wikispaces:** www.wikispaces.com

**Wetpaint:** www.wetpaint.com

**Tip**
Wiki means "quick" in the Hawaiian language. Some wikis only allow certain users to edit information on the site.

Activity 9

# Video-Sharing Sites

Easy to Modify for Younger Kids

## Goal

Your child will watch an online video and then write a review.

## Materials

- computer with Internet access
- paper and pencil

## Steps

### 1. Prepare

Locate and screen for appropriateness one or more videos for your child to watch from video-sharing sites such as YouTube (www.youtube.com). Choose videos related to topics that your child is interested in, such as a favorite book, TV show, music, or school subject. You might want to explore sites that have videos just for kids such as Totlol (www.totlol.com) or TeacherTube (www.teachertube.com) or other video sites that share your values. You may want to create an account on YouTube and store certain videos that are appropriate for your child.

### 2. Watch

Allow your child to watch the video or videos. You could have your child take notes, or just watch for fun.

### 3. Write

After watching the video or videos, have your child write a short paragraph explaining whether he liked or did not like the video including reasons why or why not.

**Tip**
Consider using software, such as Safe Eyes (www.safeeyes.com), that filters online videos for inappropriate content. Clearly define to your child your expectations for watching videos online.

Activity **10**

# Make a Book

Easy to
Modify for
Younger Kids

## Goal

Your child will make a book on the 16 Web 2.0 terms and concepts learned throughout this chapter.

## Materials

- markers or colored pencils
- white paper (any size or style)
- stapler
- construction paper (optional)
- stickers (optional)

## Steps

### 1. Draw

Have your child draw an illustration of one of the Web 2.0 terms located at the beginning of the chapter on a piece of blank paper. For example, for blogging, your child might draw a picture of a keyboard.

### 2. Label

Have your child label the illustration by writing the vocabulary term on the paper. Allow her to be creative and write it anywhere on the paper.

### 3. Purpose

Instruct your child to write the definition of the term, describing what it does. Repeat steps 1–3 for each vocabulary term.

## 4. *Decorate*

Allow your child to decorate each page using markers, colored pencils, or stickers. Your child could make a cover for the book from construction paper. Have your child staple the pages together to make a book.

## 5. *Read*

Allow your child to read the book to you or someone else.

**Tip**
Tell your child to create this book as if teaching these terms to a younger sibling or another child. This may help her while writing the definitions. She could even make up a creative story included the vocabulary and information learned in this chapter. This activity allows your child to process the information and make it her own, so if possible, allow your child to write her own meanings of the terms. She could write some other facts about the vocabulary while creating her book.

# Grade Book

(If needed, please see the Introduction for help on how to use this grade book. This grade book is also available on CD.)

**Name:** _____

Paste or draw a picture of your choice in the space below.

## Chapter 1 **Computer Basics**

| Activities | Date | Grade |
|---|---|---|
| 1. Computer Basics Slide Show | | |
| 2. Online Research | | |
| 3. Identify the Devices | | |
| 4. Make a Book | | |
| 5. Website Scavenger Hunt | | |
| 6. Coloring Book | | |
| 7. Computer Device Cards | | |
| 8. Design a Computer System | | |
| 9. Slide Show Quiz | | |
| 10. Quiz | | |

Chapter Average: _____

Chapter Grade: _____

## Chapter 2 **Safety on the Internet**

| Activities | Date | Grade |
|---|---|---|
| 1. Internet Safety Song | | |
| 2. Online Interactive Stories | | |
| 3. Golden Rule | | |
| 4. Internet Safety Terms | | |
| 5. Internet Safety Slide Show | | |
| 6. Treasure Hunt Game | | |
| 7. Internet Safety Games | | |
| 8. Contract | | |
| 9. Netiquette | | |
| 10. Quiz | | |

Chapter Average: _____

Chapter Grade: _____

## Chapter 3 **Keyboarding**

| Activities | Date | Grade |
|---|---|---|
| 1. Keyboarding Position | | |
| 2. Learn the Keys | | |
| 3. Keyboard Chart | | |
| 4. Keyboard Styles | | |
| 5. WPM | | |
| 6. Practive Typing | | |
| 7. Keboard Chart Game | | |
| 8. Typing Game | | |
| 9. Quiz | | |
| 10. Test | | |

Chapter Average: _____

Chapter Grade: _____

## Chapter 4 **The World Wide Web**

| Activities | Date | Grade |
|---|---|---|
| 1. World Wide Web Slide Show | | |
| 2. Internet Tutorials | | |
| 3. URL Worksheet | | |
| 4. URL Cards | | |
| 5. Web Browsers | | |
| 6. Internet Dramatization | | |
| 7. Internet Protocol (IP) Address | | |
| 8. Internet Connection Speeds | | |
| 9. Switches and Hubs | | |
| 10. Quiz | | |

Chapter Average: _____

Chapter Grade: _____

## Chapter 5 **Word Processing**

| Activities | Date | Grade |
|---|---|---|
| 1. Word Processing Icons | | |
| 2. Word Processing Tutorials | | |
| 3. Skills Checklist | | |
| 4. Documents | | |
| 5. Poem | | |
| 6. Recipe | | |
| 7. Greeting Card | | |
| 8. Word Search | | |
| 9. Newsletter | | |
| 10. Quiz | | |

Chapter Average: _____

Chapter Grade: _____

## Chapter 6 **Internet Research**

| Activities | Date | Grade |
|---|---|---|
| 1. Search Engines | | |
| 2. Bird Research | | |
| 3. Ocean Animal Research | | |
| 4. Natural Hazard Cards | | |
| 5. Natural Hazards Research | | |
| 6. Weather Bear | | |
| 7. Weather Chart | | |
| 8. Choose a Topic | | |
| 9. Create a Slide | | |
| 10. Slide Presentation | | |

Chapter Average: _____

Chapter Grade: _____

## Chapter 7 **Peripheral Devices**

| Activities | Date | Grade |
|---|---|---|
| 1. Peripheral Devices Slide Show | | |
| 2. Internet Research | | |
| 3. Identify the Devices | | |
| 4. Make a Book | | |
| 5. Website Scavenger Hunt | | |
| 6. Coloring Book | | |
| 7. Peripheral Device Cards | | |
| 8. Input: Output: Storage | | |
| 9. Matching Game | | |
| 10. Quiz | | |

Chapter Average: _____

Chapter Grade: _____

## Chapter 8 **Communicating Using the Internet**

| Activities | Date | Grade |
|---|---|---|
| 1. E-mail Slide Show | | |
| 2. How E-mail Works | | |
| 3. Send an E-mail | | |
| 4. Instant Messaging Slide Show | | |
| 5. Send an Instant Message (IM) | | |
| 6. Emoticons and Acronyms Slide Show | | |
| 7. Emoticons and Acronyms Quiz | | |
| 8. VoIP and Videoconferencing Slide Show | | |
| 9. VoIP Phone Call | | |
| 10. Videoconference | | |

Chapter Average: _____

Chapter Grade: _____

## Chapter 9  Multimedia Presentations

| Activities | Date | Grade |
|---|---|---|
| 1. Online Stories | | |
| 2. Word Search | | |
| 3. Sample Slide Show | | |
| 4. Slide Show Tutorials | | |
| 5. Storyboard | | |
| 6. Storyboard Self-Assessment | | |
| 7. Create a Slide Show | | |
| 8. Rehearse | | |
| 9. Slide Show Presentation | | |
| 10. Make a Book | | |

Chapter Average: _____

Chapter Grade: _____

## Chapter 10  Graphs and Spreadsheets

| Activities | Date | Grade |
|---|---|---|
| 1. Graph Slide Show | | |
| 2. Graph Worksheet | | |
| 3. Draw a Graph | | |
| 4. Create a Graph Online | | |
| 5. Spreadsheets | | |
| 6. Spreadsheet Tutorials | | |
| 7. Graphing with a Spreadsheet | | |
| 8. Formulas | | |
| 9. Sorting | | |
| 10. Quiz | | |

Chapter Average: _____

Chapter Grade: _____

## Chapter 11 **Inside a Computer**

| Activities | Date | Grade |
|---|---|---|
| 1. Computer Parts Slide Show | | |
| 2. Internet Research | | |
| 3. Identify the Computer Parts | | |
| 4. Make a Book | | |
| 5. Website Scavenger Hunt | | |
| 6. Computer Part Cards | | |
| 7. Matching Game | | |
| 8. Troubleshooting Computer Errors | | |
| 9. Cords and Cables | | |
| 10. Quiz | | |

Chapter Average: _____

Chapter Grade: _____

## Chapter 12 **Web 2.0 Activities**

| Activities | Date | Grade |
|---|---|---|
| 1. Blog Slide Show | | |
| 2. Blogging | | |
| 3. Blog Quiz | | |
| 4. Podcast Slide Show | | |
| 5. RSS Feeds | | |
| 6. Podcasting | | |
| 7. Podcast Quiz | | |
| 8. Wiki | | |
| 9. Video-Sharing Sites | | |
| 10. Make a Book | | |

Chapter Average: _____

Chapter Grade: _____

# National Educational Technology Standards for Students (NET•S)

All K–12 students should be prepared to meet the following standards and performance indicators.

1.  **Creativity and Innovation**

    Students demonstrate creative thinking, construct knowledge, and develop innovative products and processes using technology. Students:

    a.  apply existing knowledge to generate new ideas, products, or processes

    b.  create original works as a means of personal or group expression

    c.  use models and simulations to explore complex systems and issues

    d.  identify trends and forecast possibilities

2.  **Communication and Collaboration**

    Students use digital media and environments to communicate and work collaboratively, including at a distance, to support individual learning and contribute to the learning of others. Students:

    a.  interact, collaborate, and publish with peers, experts, or others employing a variety of digital environments and media

    b.  communicate information and ideas effectively to multiple audiences using a variety of media and formats

    c.  develop cultural understanding and global awareness by engaging with learners of other cultures

    d.  contribute to project teams to produce original works or solve problems

3. **Research and Information Fluency**

   Students apply digital tools to gather, evaluate, and use information. Students:

   a. plan strategies to guide inquiry

   b. locate, organize, analyze, evaluate, synthesize, and ethically use information from a variety of sources and media

   c. evaluate and select information sources and digital tools based on the appropriateness to specific tasks

   d. process data and report results

4. **Critical Thinking, Problem Solving, and Decision Making**

   Students use critical-thinking skills to plan and conduct research, manage projects, solve problems, and make informed decisions using appropriate digital tools and resources. Students:

   a. identify and define authentic problems and significant questions for investigation

   b. plan and manage activities to develop a solution or complete a project

   c. collect and analyze data to identify solutions and make informed decisions

   d. use multiple processes and diverse perspectives to explore alternative solutions

5. **Digital Citizenship**

   Students understand human, cultural, and societal issues related to technology and practice legal and ethical behavior. Students:

   a. advocate and practice the safe, legal, and responsible use of information and technology

   b. exhibit a positive attitude toward using technology that supports collaboration, learning, and productivity

   c. demonstrate personal responsibility for lifelong learning

   d. exhibit leadership for digital citizenship

6. **Technology Operations and Concepts**

Students demonstrate a sound understanding of technology concepts, systems, and operations. Students:

   a.  understand and use technology systems

   b.  select and use applications effectively and productively

   c.  troubleshoot systems and applications

   d.  transfer current knowledge to the learning of new technologies